the teenage guy's survival guide

the teenage guy's survival guide

by jeremy daldry

LITTLE, BROWN AND COMPANY
New York   Boston

Little, Brown and Company • Hachette Book Group
237 Park Avenue, New York, NY 10017 • Visit our website at www.lb-teens.com

Little, Brown and Company is a division of Hachette Book Group, Inc.
The Little, Brown name and logo are trademarks of Hachette Book Group, Inc.

The publisher is not responsible for websites (or their content) that are not owned by the publisher.

First U.S. Edition: May 1999
First published in Great Britain by Piccadilly Press

Photograph on page 10, © 1995 Michael Krasowitz/FPG; photograph on page 67, © 1997 Chip Simons/FPG; photograph on page 90, © 1997 Arthur Tilley/FPG; photograph on page 105, © 1997 Michael Krasowitz/FPG. Illustrations by Adam Chiu.

LIBRARY OF CONGRESS CATALOGING-IN-PUBLICATION DATA
Daldry, Jeremy
        The teenage guy's survival guide / by Jeremy Daldry.
            p.   cm.
        Edited and rev. ed. of: Boys behaving badly, 1997.
        Includes bibliography references.
        Summary: A humorous guide for boys ages ten to fourteen, offering advice on dating, sex, body changes, and social life.
            ISBN 978-0-316-17824-2
        1. Teenage boys — United States — Juvenile literature. 2. Adolescence — Juvenile literature. 3. Puberty — Juvenile literature. 4. Interpersonal relations in adolescence — Juvenile literature. [1. Teenage boys. 2. Puberty. 3. Sex instruction for boys.] I. Daldry, Jeremy, Boys behaving badly. II. Title
HQ797.D35   1999
305.235 — dc21   98-40816

20 19 18 17 16 15 14 13 12 11

RRD-C

Printed in the United States of America

 DEDICATION

This book is dedicated,
with love and admiration,
to my father.

Contents

PLUMBING (Masturbation, Wet Dreams)

SEXY THOUGHTS (Magazines)

three

four

Arrrrrrgh! What? Where? When? Who?

WHAT'S HAPPENING TO ME?

Take a deep breath. Relax. Don't panic.

It's called being a **teenager.**

And it's perfectly normal.

And besides, that's why you (or someone else) have bought this

excellent, and **PRETTY FUNNY,** book —

to help answer those pesky, silly questions and offer you a user's guide to

being a teenage guy.

So, what's this book all about, then?

Girls, mainly.

And — dates, kissing, conquests, dumping, being dumped, broken

hearts, crushes, shaving, zits, greasy hair, being stinky, masturbation, wet

dreams, success, failure, depression, confidence, listening, talking, drinking,

drugs, peer pressure, bullying, fighting, parents, clothes, friends, money.

Oh, and girls.

Cool!

Chapter One

Surviving Love and Sex

What Are Girls Like?

They are just great.  There is something about them that is just so very squeezable. *You bet they are. I LOVE girls!*

short girls, TALL girls, **fat** girls . . . THIN girls

They're all great. We love them.

But that doesn't stop girls from being the cause of more heartache, confusion, and sleepless nights than almost anything else.

They might be wonderful — but they are also weird. All that giggling, drooling over rock stars, and doing their nails and hair. What is that all about?

And as for trying to talk to them . . .

It's been scientifically proven that when any guy gets within two feet of a girl, she gives off a mysterious aura that turns a normal guy into a gibbering wreck who can't string two words together.

**It's proven. It's science. Strange but true.
But you still want to talk to them.
You want to be close to them.
You want to hold their hands,
and go out on dates with them.**

 Ywohtz hibby brb?

And kiss them, and cuddle them,
and kiss them, and kiss them some more.

And therein lies a very **BIG** problem: asking a girl out on a date.

Even when it's totally obvious that a girl has a huge crush on you, why do you find it so hard just to go up and ask her out?

I'll tell you why.

Because of the big **N. O.**

Because you're scared of being rejected or that the girl in question will tell her friends, who then will all have a good laugh about you.

But it shouldn't be scary, because, let's face it: You probably know when a girl wants to be asked out.

No, you do, really.

Does she wear a T-shirt that says "Ask me out"?

There are those funny little signs. Like?

Well, when you talk to the girl in question:

- **She blushes, or she starts to play with her hair.**
- **She smiles when she sees you coming and "accidentally" touches you on the hand or leg when you leave.**
- **She laughs at your lame jokes, asks lots of questions about you, and then listens really closely to whatever you've got to say.**

There are tons and tons of little signs. You've just got to watch for them.

But wait a minute.

What is so wrong with a *girl* asking one of us *guys* out for a night on the town or a walk in the park?

Nothing. Absolutely nothing. There is no rule that says that girls can't ask boys out. They should. It makes us feel wanted and means that for once we guys don't have to go through the pre-ask-out-on-a-date

hell.

So, if there are any GIRLS reading this book, take a hint:

Ask more boys out.

Attention!

WE LIKE IT!

But back to you and your potential date . . .

Asking a Girl Out

Here is a big tip: Supposedly surefire lines like:

"Baby, it's your lucky day,"

"What's a beautiful girl like you doing in a place like this?"

"Hey, gorgeous, where have you been all my life?"

or

Hey — these are all my best lines!

will only guarantee that you end up spending an awful lot of time ALONE. Girls might want to be asked out, but they don't want to be insulted.

So, there is nothing to do but take a deep breath, walk up to your date target and say something like, **"Would you like to go out with me on Saturday night?"**

Maybe it's not the most subtle or clever of things to say, but sometimes the direct approach is best.

[HERE'S A SECRET]

You want to be a little sneaky about it? Don't ask — *suggest* a date.

What's the difference?

Well, **"Want to go to the movies with me?"** will get you a **YES** or **NO** answer.

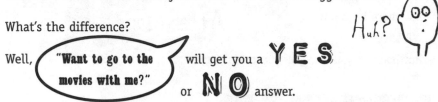

Which is great if the girl says YES and not so great if she says NO.

But if you say, **"I've got a couple of tickets for the movies. I thought I might give you one,"**

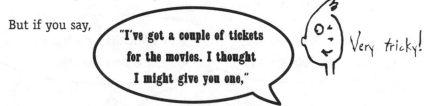

you're not forcing the issue — you're easing into it.

It's subtle, it's cute, and it works.

And before you ask, *think* about what you are going to do on your date.

Make out, I hope!

It's sometimes best, when you ask someone out, to give her some options, or at least give a hint at what the date might be. But if you plan your date in too much detail before you ask, you won't have any flexibility to change your plans.

So instead of

> "I thought we could meet in town at 1600 hours, inspect the local retail outlets until 1645 hours, and then retire to the moving-picture complex to watch the 1700-hours feature,"

you could try

> "If you want, we could meet in town at around four and then maybe catch a movie."

Safer still is

> "Want to meet at the mall around four and then decide what to do?"

That will give you the chance to check out what's happening that afternoon and plan a few different things.

SOME BASIC ASKING-OUT RULES:

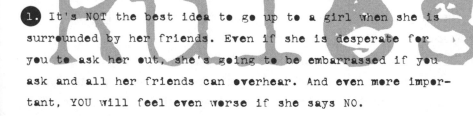

1. It's NOT the best idea to go up to a girl when she is surrounded by her friends. Even if she is desperate for you to ask her out, she's going to be embarrassed if you ask and all her friends can overhear. And even more important, YOU will feel even worse if she says NO.

2. GET to the point. Don't "ummm" and "uhhh." Don't spend hours leading up to asking her out. Just say hi, ask her how she's doing, and then come out with "If you're free on Saturday night..."

3. DON'T, don't, don't get a friend to ask for you. That's just so tacky. Remember that you are asking a girl out because you want to be with her — no other reason. If you get a friend to ask her out, it looks like you don't really care that much whether she says YES or NO, and it makes you look like a complete coward. Also, your friend might move in on your date and ask her out himself!

Hey, I never thought of that....

RiNG

RiNG

RiNG

RiNG

And for those of you who really want to go for the safe option, you just need a phone. Some people are more relaxed on the phone. They find it easier to talk. Can't face the girl in the flesh? Call her.

But don't BLURT it out and don't TAKE FOREVER to get to the point. Why not write a few notes outlining what you want to say before you say it? It's not dorky, and she won't be able to tell. Then just pick a good time to call:

- *not too early in the morning*
- *not too late at night*
- *not when there is a great movie on TV which she might be watching,*

and

GO FOR IT.

Yeah, like 11:30 P.M., when Sleepless in Seattle is on.

But if you do use the phone,

remember to ask to speak to your potential date and say who's calling.

People can sound different on the phone, and you don't want this to happen:

"Hi, Cindy. I was wondering if you'd like to go out to the movies with me on Saturday."

"I think you want to speak to my daughter."

"Oh, sorry. Yes, please." (Embarrassing pause.)

"Hi, this is Cindy."

"Hi, Cindy. I was just wondering if you'd like to go out to the movies with me on Saturday."

"That sounds nice — but who is this?"

Not the best way to start a date.

D·oh!

It's really simple: You want to ask; your date probably wants to be asked. So take your time, get to know the person, smile, be confident, walk up to her, and ask her out.

Hello, girl. Erm . . . wanna go on a date?

What to Do If She Says No

If the girl in question does say, "Thanks, but no thanks," there is no point pleading, getting down on your knees, or getting all huffy about it. If you ask someone out, she has the right to say no.

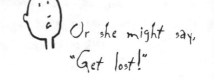

DON'T   TAKE IT PERSONALLY,
DON'T   GET DEPRESSED BY IT, and
DON'T   STORM OFF IN A HUFF.

Or she might say, "Get lost!"

It happens to everyone. You'll get over it. Sometimes you'll get knocked back, and that can be annoying. Even the biggest dude in the entire world has been rejected sometimes. But if you never ask, you'll never know, and you could be missing out on some red-hot dates.

No problem — I'll just have a fun Saturday night with the guys. Who needs girls anyway?

The Date

OK, so you managed to get up the nerve to actually ask the girl of your dreams out on a date. But now you've actually got to GO ON THE DATE.

What?

How?

Where?

When?

Argggghh!!!

Don't panic. Take a deep breath. Chill out.

Landing on the moon might seem simple compared to planning a good first date. But don't worry, because it's really easy. *Yeah, right!*

And remember, you're not the only one who's freaking out about the whole thing. She will almost certainly be going through exactly the same stomach-turning, last-minute panic.

Everyone thinks it's just girls who spend all day preparing for dates. No way!

We've all done it: sat there trying to decide what to wear, spent so long in the bathroom that your mom comes and knocks on the door and says if you don't stop whatever you're doing, you'll go blind, and even stolen some of your dad's aftershave so you smell like a love god.

I've never done that!

And that's before you've even left the house!

So, first big decision:

What to Wear

OK, let's start with:

What NOT to Wear

- *There is no point borrowing your brother's latest club clothes, because if you get as far as a second date, your potential girlfriend might expect you to wear something equally hip. Also, if you "borrow" something from your older brother without asking him, you might have to go on your date minus the hip outfit but plus a black eye.*
- *Don't buy something new. If you blow all your cash on a new outfit and then next time you see your date, you are dressed like a loser, you'll look stupid.*

T-shirt, 4 weeks old; ripped jeans; old sneakers with holes in the toe — how much cooler can you get?

- *Don't wear a tie. I mean, come on, a tie! You're not going to your cousin's wedding.**

* Unless, of course, your date *is* at your cousin's wedding — then maybe a tie might be a good idea.

Good Things to Wear

You want to look like you care — like you've made an effort to make yourself look good for your date.

But you should always wear something that makes you feel comfortable.

Studly, scruffy, whatever . . . as long as it's YOU, it really shouldn't matter. Remember, she's going on a date with YOU, not your wardrobe.

And while we are on the subject of things to wear and not to wear, let's talk about aftershave.

> **Half a bottle of Brut down your boxers does NOT smell good. It will also hurt like crazy, so don't do it.**

Ouch, ouch! Too late!

Girls like you to smell nice, so wash your feet, but they don't like you to smell like the perfume counter at Macy's, so remember, a little goes a long way.

So you smell nice, you look cool, everything is great. Let's get on to the date itself.

How to Behave on the Date

What would YOU know?

You might know this girl really well — she might be your best friend — but you've never been on a date with her before. And dates are different. Don't ask me why — they just are. You've asked a girl out
TO BE WITH YOU.
ALONE.
BECAUSE YOU LIKE HER.   Oh, my God — now what?

But remember: Relax, relax, relax. You have asked a girl out on a date, and she has said YES.

She wants to be there.

She wants to be with you.

She must like you at least a little.

Not a bad place to start a date from.

*I do a great Donald Duck.
quack, quack, flap, flap.
Good, isn't it?*

THINGS TO REMEMBER:

Don't Forget

1. Be on time.

You've asked her out and it will not go over well if you
are late.

BUT WHAT IF THE GIRL YOU HAVE ASKED OUT IS LATE?
Well, it's only polite to wait a while. You never know —
she might have been held up or missed her bus.

BUT HOW LONG SHOULD YOU WAIT? AND WHAT SHOULD YOU DO
WHILE YOU ARE WAITING?
Twenty minutes is about the minimum you should wait —
although if you really like the girl, you might find yourself hanging around for at least an hour. If you have
arranged to meet someone, it's usually a good idea to have
a book or a magazine with you, and then if she is late,
you can read. There is nothing worse than waiting on a
street corner for someone and feeling like everyone knows
you are waiting on a street corner for someone.

An hour! You've got to be kidding me!

2. Have an idea where to go.

Ideally you will have already covered what you are going to do on your date when you asked her out, but if you didn't, have at least a couple of suggestions up your sleeve.

You don't want this to happen:

Kiss?

You: "What do you want to do?"

Your date: "I dunno, what do you want to do?"

You: "Whatever."

Your date: "I don't mind, whatever you feel like."

You: "I'm easy. It's up to you."

Your date: "Whatever. You pick."

Hey! How did you know what happens when I go out on a date?

You: "Nah, you."

I mean, please. Something like this might be a little better:

You: "What do you want to do?"

Your date: "I don't know, what do you want to do?"

23

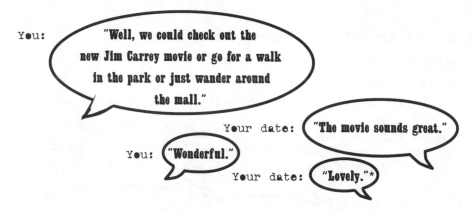

"Well, we could check out the new Jim Carrey movie or go for a walk in the park or just wander around the mall."

Your date: "The movie sounds great."

You: "Wonderful."

Your date: "Lovely."*

*If you really talk like this you are: a) straight out of a cheesy Harlequin romance novel b) in need of more help than this little book can offer c) Prince Charles.

Another way of tackling the whole "what to do?" thing might be to let your date choose.

Always remember: YOU ASKED HER OUT.

If she doesn't mind and leaves it up to you, then pick something you will both enjoy.

First dates that take place at the nearest video arcade are usually also last dates. Unless, of course, your date is really into video games.

Movies are a pretty safe bet. There is probably something playing that you would both like to see, and it also means that you can spend time together without having to talk the whole time.

- *No embarrassing pauses in conversation.*
- *No trying to think of what to say next.*
- *And you'll have something to talk about afterward.*

But remember, just because you want to see <u>REVENGE OF THE NUNS IN CHAIN-SAW HELL, PART FOUR,</u>

A classic movie — but not as good as "Mutant Toxic Bikini Girls Go Splat."

doesn't mean your date will want to. Ask her what she would like to see.

Blah, blah, blah, blah, blah, blah, blah, blah, blah, blah, blah, blah, blah.

3. Talk.

Whatever you end up doing with your date, you are going to have to talk to her at some point.

It can't be helped — that's what dates are all about.

Talking to a date might seem a little daunting. It can be difficult; it can seem embarrassing; you might think you are sounding stupid. And nerves can get the better of you.

You might want to say,

"That was a good movie, wasn't it?"

But what might come out is,

"Wibble, yipple, pipple, pong, belch."

Just relax. Here's a secret: GIRLS ARE PEOPLE, TOO. They will forgive you if you get your words backward or if you make a bad joke. They are as nervous as you are.

But if you are worried about these **L O N G,** embarrassing pauses, just remember to follow a few simple rules:

- **Listen to her. There is no point thinking up something witty to say if you haven't been paying any attention to what she has been saying.**
- **Don't bore her. She isn't out with you to be lectured at about why Brett Favre is a football god, how Motorhead rocks, or why Pamela Anderson is every guy's dream girl.**

Blah, blah, blah, blah, blah, blah, blah, blah . . .
Hello? Hello?   ZZZZZZZZZZZZ

- **Don't go on and on and on and on and on and on about yourself, either. The whole point of a good conversation is that it goes two ways. It's fine to drop in little things about yourself, but don't sit down and tell her your life story — unless, of course, she asks.**

I was born on a dark and stormy night . . .

- **Ask her questions. Most people like, and are good at, talking about themselves. It will also show that you are interested in her and want to find out more. It's also a good idea to ask questions that don't require just a yes-or-no answer. So asking,**

"Which part of the movie did you like best?"

is better than asking,

"That was a good movie, wasn't it?"

- *Share some secrets. The fastest way to get to know someone better is to tell her something about you that is personal and not obvious. Letting her know you were sad about your grandmother dying or that your favorite thing to do on a rainy day is to stay in re-reading* The Catcher in the Rye *tells her something special about you. On the other hand, you don't want to scare her away by getting too intimate too quickly. (Recounting the hot dream you had about her last night is probably NOT a good idea.)*
- *Don't rush to fill every breath with a joke or a story. Every conversation has some silences.*
- *Relax. The whole point of a date is that you are trying someone on for size — seeing if she fits, seeing if you hit it off, seeing if you like each other enough to go on another date and another and another.*

Oh, sure. That's easy for you to say.

4. Think About the Money Question Beforehand.

This is a tough one. No girl should expect you to pay for everything.

Cash, dinero, dough, moola.

If you want to pay for your date, that's fine — that's your privilege, but no girl should expect it to be her right.

If you are going to the movies, you might want to offer to pay — most girls will then pick up a pizza afterward or buy some popcorn.

Don't, don't, don't tell a girl you would like to take her out and then turn up broke and have to resort to a hot date sitting in a bus shelter. If you've got no cash, then let her know subtly when you ask her out. Suggest a walk in the park and an ice cream — cheap, cool, and pretty romantic.

> **Remember: You don't have to have great wads of cash to go on a good date.**

5. Don't forget you are on a date with her.

If you run into some buddies, don't go off with them and ignore your date. However, if you do see someone you know, don't try to hide the fact that you are on a date.

If you act like you are embarrassed to be with your date, it will probably be your last date with her. But don't parade her around, either. She isn't a trophy or a new pair of sneakers for your friends to admire and make comments about.

Do any of these things and you will, to be frank, look like a jerk. And your date will hate it.

6. Offer to walk your date home.

It's only polite and shows that you care that she gets home safely. But if she says she'll be OK, don't, don't, don't make a big deal about how dangerous the streets are and how you must protect her. You're not Superman; she's not Lois Lane. The days of knights in shining armor are long gone. Chances are she's comfortable in her neighborhood and can look after herself.

So, everything has gone well. You've had a great date. She's

- *laughed at your jokes,*
- *listened to your stories,*
- *enjoyed the movie, and*
- *shared a milk shake with you at McDonald's.*

You are a success. The date is a success. But now comes the biggest problem of all . . .

The Kiss Goodnight

It's about time!

Wow — that's always a real toughie . . .

When?

Where?

How?

Tongues or no tongues?

But what if my breath smells, our teeth clank, or our noses get all smooshed?

But **don't panic:**

The kiss good night can be really nice and not as nerve-racking as you might think.

The difficult thing about the kiss good night is that someone has to make the first move; otherwise you'll never get around to touching lips or tickling tongues.

So, this is the scene:

The date's been great, and you've walked the girl to her bus stop or her house.

And then you stop.

You say thanks for coming.

Your date says thanks for a great time.

You both stand and do a swirly, twisty little dance on the spot.

You both look at each other.

You both giggle a little and then . . .

NOTHING.

But that's where a kiss should come in.

Hey — I've been there before.

So, what do you do?

Well, while you are giggling and twirling, you could reach out your hand. Your date might understand what you are trying to do, and take it.

Wow — you've touched. Pretty electric stuff.

Zowee!

And then just let your hand, still holding hers, fall to your side. Now, unless you've both got incredibly **s t r e t c h y** arms, you're going to have to move closer together.

We are not talking about pulling your date to you like a fish on the end of a line — just letting your hand and arm suggest a movement that gets your date closer to you.

How close?

About the length of your lips.

Now is the time for courage.

That's close.

The time for the **KiSS.**

Reach in gently and plant a delicate kiss on your date's lips or, if you want to take it more slowly, her cheek. You'll then know dead certain whether she wants you to kiss her again, because if she does, she'll kiss you back.

It's all very simple. The key is reading the signals — those little signals that let you know when the time is right and whether your date wants to be kissed at all.

All the:

- *giggling,*
- *looking into each other's eyes,*
- *holding hands,*
- *gently touching each other's arms or backs.*

Little things like these. And when you get to the moment of truth, you'll find:

- *your face very close to hers,*
- *yourselves looking into each other's eyes,*
- *that the conversation has dried up,*
- *you both glancing at each other's mouth,*
- *yourselves kissing.*

Wow.

Yippee.

Home run.

Houston, we have touched down.

However, if there isn't any giggling, your date is walking quickly ahead of you with her arms crossed, and any conversation is of the "Yes," "No," variety, then there probably isn't going to be a kiss.

Hey — I've been there before, too!

Don't take it personally — sometimes dates just don't work out. If that's the case, it's time to bow out and admit that it wasn't meant to be. No hard feelings.

Or perhaps your date just doesn't feel ready to kiss you yet. If you've obviously gotten along well, then she'd probably still like to go on another date. Remember to read those signs. Each situation is different.

But let's say that the date is a success and the kiss is fast looming. We come to that eternal question: To tongue or not to tongue?

Sometimes people like to kiss with their mouths open and use their tongues to explore each other's mouths. As gross as that sounds, it actually feels very nice, although it might take a little bit of getting used to. It's called French kissing — although it has nothing to do with the French. If you don't want to French-kiss, or your date doesn't want to, then there is no rule that says you have to.

Je t'aime, wee, wee, ooh, la, la — wanna kiss?

Kissing isn't a simple matter of *A, B, C.*

Sometimes a quick LIP LOCK is wonderful; sometimes an end-of-the-world TASTY TONGUE KISS is the only thing that will do. But on your first kiss good night, it's probably best to err on the side of caution.

Just remember these basic kissing rules, which apply just as well for the first kiss good night as for any other time you kiss a girl.

- **Don't** *lunge at the girl as if you are trying to tackle her.*
- **Don't** *try to force your tongue as far down her throat as it will go. You're kissing, not trying to find out what she had for lunch.*
- **Don't** *assume that just because you've been out on a date, you have the right to kiss her. You don't. And your date doesn't have the right to kiss you or expect you to kiss her, either.*
- **Don't** *assume that just because you've had a quick kiss, things are automatically going to go further.*
- **Do** *pick your place — somewhere that isn't too busy and where neither her friends nor yours will suddenly make an appearance.*
- **Do** *make sure, if it's outside your date's house, that her parents can't see. She might feel uncomfortable about having a quick kiss with her mom watching through the window.*
- **Do** *take your time.*
- **Do** *enjoy it.*

Dates can be a nightmare, but they don't have to be. From asking a girl out to kissing her good night, the key to the whole thing is to take your time, be yourself, and never, ever forget that you are with another person — not a cardboard cutout but a real person who has **interests,** *feelings,* and **EMOTIONS** just like you.

If it doesn't work out — don't worry about it. It happens. Sometimes two people who should get along like a house on fire can't stand each other after they've spent some time together alone.

Just move on.

Always remember that every great romantic duo, every old married couple, and every movie star, rock god, or super model has all had first dates.

Relax — enjoy them.

The Next Step

The date has gone great.

You had a kiss good night.

You are totally psyched because

A GIRL LIKES YOU.

Excellent. Congratulations.

Now what?

Thank you very much!
It was nothing, really.

Well, going into school the next day and telling all your friends that you made out with so-and-so from history class is a big no-no.

But all my friends ask me for details!

Why?

Look, just think about it for a minute.

It's natural to feel great if you really hit it off with someone — you feel happy and even proud.

It's natural to want to tell as many people as possible so they'll all know how happy you are and maybe even so you can brag about it a little bit.

But remember that you are talking about SOMEONE ELSE — and someone else who you supposedly like.

The other person might not want the

whole school,

basketball team,

world

to know that you had a quick kiss in the park and that you tried to put your hand up her shirt.

If you make out with someone, it's always best to assume that she wants to keep it a secret. When you first start seeing a girl, when you first become an item, it takes a little while for you both to get used to the idea.

It takes a while for you to stop going,

> "Wow. I am actually going out with her. I can't believe it."

And oddly enough, that's why when we first start dating someone, we want to tell other people — because it makes it all seem more real to us.

CONFUSED?

HERE'S HOW IT GOES:

1. You go out on a date with Little Miss Gorgeous.
2. You and LMG make out with each other.
3. You and LMG decide to become boyfriend and girlfriend.
4. You can't believe that you and LMG are going out — because she is so gorgeous.

5. You tell all your friends about going out with LMG because that makes it more real. If your friends know, it must be true.

6. LMG dumps you because she didn't want anyone to know right away.

BUMMER.

If you really are bursting to tell someone, then just tell one friend who you can trust not to spread the news around. Better still, write it down in a diary or a letter to yourself.

Dear Me,
I'm going out with a gorgeous girl. She is gorgeous.
I can't believe it — but now that I've written it down,
it must be true. Wow.
Sincerely,
Me

Hey!! That's private!

Simple.

So, once you've both gotten used to the idea that you are an item, then it might be nice to let people know that you are a couple. You don't have to take out an ad in the local paper. Just hold hands in public, be seen together, snuggle together.

People will get the idea.

However, if you are dating a girl and after a few weeks or even a few months, she still doesn't want people to know that you are together, then it might be a good idea to ask why.

Just as it's not natural to rush out and put up posters announcing that you're an item, it's also not natural never to tell anyone.

It might mean that she isn't happy about something, she might feel a little embarrassed, or she might just be very shy. Not everyone likes to live their private lives in public.

BUZZ, CRACKLE ... this is WKSS with an important news flash. I have a new babe. We repeat, I have a new girlfriend.

If you want to go public and she doesn't, sit and talk about it. There is probably a very good reason. Remember, talking is the best thing you can ever do with a girl. Well, maybe not the best thing — but we'll talk about that later.

Nudge, nudge, wink, wink, say no more.

Making a Relationship Work

(Batteries not included)

(Also known as BEING ROMANTIC)

Just because you've gone out with a girl a few times doesn't mean you can sit back on your heels and relax. The toughest challenge is yet to come.

You've got to make your relationship work.

How do you do that?

Well, with something that guys of all ages find difficult, embarrassing, and sometimes downright impossible. It's called *romance.*

Is that flowers and stuff?

Romance is very important, because when the romance goes, your whole relationship begins to fizzle.

IT'S TRUE.

You can lust after someone, love them so much you feel like you're floating, but the day the romance dies is the day the clock is counting down to the big split between the two of you.

So, how do you capture the romance of a relationship and keep it? Well, here's a home truth — you meet someone, you fall in love, and everything that girl says and does is romantic. SHE CAN BURP, FART, OR THROW UP, AND YOU'LL THINK IT'S CUTE, ENDEARING, AND SWEET.

But once you've been with someone a little bit longer, that's when the romance can begin to disappear — when you know exactly what your gorgeous girlfriend is about to say, do, or even think.

Yuck — no way!

And that's when you've got to roll up your sleeves and start working at romance, because if you don't nurture your relationship it will stick its little legs in the air, roll over, and kick the bucket.

So, What Is Romance?

Just what is romantic?

Anything.

Everything.

Does this mean I have to call her Snuggles?

All the expected stuff — *flowers*, **chocolates**, *love letters*. That's all romantic.

But remember, if you are being romantic, keep it simple. A single flower can be just as romantic as a huge bunch of roses and a massive box of chocolates. In fact, if you go too far overboard, it can become embarrassing, and instead of being flattered or touched, your girlfriend will feel awkward and uncomfortable.

The key to real romance is to use your head. That's why a bologna sandwich and can of soda at the right time, in the right place, with the right person, can be so much more romantic than a four-course meal in a fancy restaurant.

Romance is at its best when it's simple and when there has been some thought put into it. Anyone, if they've got the cash, can take a girl to the movies, buy her chocolates, and then whisk her off to dinner. That's not true romance — that's just easy.

True romance is all about creating or giving something special to someone you love that only the two of you will understand. That's why a plastic frog — if your loved one is crazy about **PLASTIC FROGS—** can be just as romantic as a diamond ring. *And a lot cheaper, too!*

What else is romantic?

Well, it doesn't have to involve the giving of gifts. Just taking time to be with someone can be romantic. It's very easy when you've been with some-one for a while to take them for granted — to forget just how special they are and how lucky you are to be with them. Telling someone just how much you love them is the most romantic thing. But . . .

- **walking in the park,**
- **sitting on a beach in the middle of winter,**
- **telling stories,**
- **sharing jokes and secrets, and**
- **just cuddling up and burying your face in her hair for hours**

can also be very romantic.

BUT BE CAREFUL.

Some guys get it all wrong and are romantic *all the time*. Do that and you'll probably end up being shown the door.

No one can stand having someone giving them gifts, sending them letters, or being lovey-dovey every moment of the day.

It would drive you crazy.

Romance should be thought about, rationed, made special — it's not something for every day.

And giving someone a bunch of flowers or walking in the park won't save your relationship if it's already over. No matter how romantic you are, if you and your girlfriend are destined to walk away from each other, you're going to no matter what. Romance won't save a relationship, but it can help to stop it from going downhill to begin with.

Romance should be fun, exciting, tingly, and wonderful. It's all about losing yourself in someone else. It's probably the best thing

No chance of a touchdown in overtime?

there is in the entire world, and you can't be in love without it. And we guys really can do it. There aren't any big secrets to being romantic — just use your imagination and keep it simple.

Love

So, What Is Love, Anyway?

That is not a simple question to answer. Love is not something that can be put into words.

Various poets, writers, and singers have spent hundreds of years trying to say what it is that makes *love, love,* what it is that makes us feel so very much for one particular person, what it is that makes us want to **laugh, sing, and dance** every time we see that person.

Hey, that's how I feel when my football team wins.

Only one thing is for sure: Love is not easy. It's not straightforward, and there are absolutely no rules about falling in love with someone.

You can meet someone and after a couple of hours you love her completely, or you can be friends with a person for years and years and then suddenly wake up one day and discover that you've fallen head over heels in love with her.

However, there are certain things that love *isn't* about:

- *It isn't about controlling someone or getting her to do something she doesn't want to do.*
- *It isn't about saying, "I love you," just to get a girl to make out with you.*
- *It isn't about trying to change someone to make her into the kind of girl you want her to be.*

How Do You Know It's Love?

Who can tell?

Sometimes you are with someone and you just know.

You look at her and you just know that she is a person you don't want to be without.

One way of being sure that you really do love someone before you tell her is to sit yourself down and ask yourself some questions.

Me: "Do I love this girl?"

Me 2: "Yes. I think so."

Me: "Are you sure, Me 2?"

Me 2: "Well, I think I'm sure."

Me: "Do you think about her a lot?"

Me 2: "All the time. I can't think of anything else."

Me: "Do you long to be with her?"

Me 2: "Oh, yes. She's great. She makes me feel kind of whole and special."

Me: "Would you feel absolutely devastated if you could never see her again?"

Me 2: "Do sour-cream-and-onion potato chips make your breath smell like the inside of an old jock strap?"

I wouldn't know —
I never eat old jockstraps.

Me: "Do you like her more than Pamela Anderson?"

Me 2: "Pamela who?"

Me: "Maybe you've just got a crush on her?"

Me 2: "Maybe. But I really know her, and I think it's more than that. I love her."

Me: "You sure you're sure?"

Me 2: "Yes. Yes, I am."

If you are being honest with yourself, you probably know in your heart of hearts whether you are really in love with someone or just have a crush on her, because one thing that love does demand is mountains of honesty.

When you are in love with someone you have to be honest with yourself and with that person. It's tough — but that's the deal.

Sometimes it's nice to think you are in love, or con yourself into thinking that you are in love, because there is nothing nicer than feeling that safe and that wanted.

But be careful not to confuse LOVE and LUST. Even though they are both exciting feelings, they *are* different. Lust tends to be purely sexual interest, while love involves deeper feelings. One good rule for telling the difference is if you like talking to her as much as you like kissing her, you might be falling in love. But if you just really like the kissing part, it might be only lust you are feeling.

So, What About Crushes?

What's the difference between being in love and having a crush? And how can we not mistake one for the other? **Who cares?**

Well, a crush is like falling in love with someone that you know you'll never get together with or someone who you don't know at all. It might be your teacher, a rock star, a supermodel, or just someone in your school.

Crushes are usually fairly intense, and the person you've got the crush on is all you can think about for a while.

But it isn't love.

What is it, then?

Crushes are based more on fantasy than anything else. It's the *idea* of that person that is so exciting.

In fact, if you and the object of your crush ever did get together, you'd probably be hugely disappointed.

Crushes are also a big part of the way that you get to understand your own particular sexuality.

When you hit puberty, it's not just your body that changes — your mind and feelings undergo a pretty major upheaval, too.

You become aware of your own sexuality, you become much more aware of girls, and you start feeling attracted to them.

Sure do!

At first it isn't always possible to understand these feelings; they can be confusing. Often you find yourself developing a crush on someone. It's usually someone older — like a teacher or a celebrity.

If you have a crush on your teacher, you do everything to please her and try to get her attention. If you have a crush on a celebrity, you might see all her movies or put up posters of her.

Give me a break!
All my teachers are REALLY old!

It's all normal, and it's all natural.

After a while things move on and you find a girlfriend or a different person to have a crush on.

You never really grow out of crushes, but they get a little less intense and a little more fun as you get older.

Saying "I Love You"

So, you've just fallen **HEAD-OVER-HEELS,** out-of-control, end-of-the-world in love with someone.

That's great.

But now you want to tell her.

That isn't so great.

Admitting that someone matters that much to you can be a particularly tough thing for us guys to do.

But it's important.

Why?

Because it's the way relationships grow — and besides, she may just feel the same way about you. Imagine you are with the girl you love. You can't help it. You're about to burst, so you tell her. And she says it back! Now, not only are you in love, but you're in love *together*.

Of course, there are all the worries and fears that when you tell her, she is going to:

a) laugh Yup. **b) slap you,** or Oh, yeah. **c) go, "What did you say?"** Very probably.

But very few girls will do any of the above.

When you tell someone that you love her, it's obvious that you are laying yourself on the line. You are being very honest and open about your feelings, and only the most heartless girl in the world would laugh at you after you've told her something so personal.

So the best thing to do is `TRUST YOUR JUDGMENT` and pick the right time to let her know just how you feel.

So don't tell her:

Like gym class?

- *over the phone*
- *in a letter*
- *just as you are saying good night*
- *after an argument*
- *when she is surrounded by her friends*
- *in a movie theater.*

Tell her somewhere that is private, but don't build the whole thing up and don't, don't, don't go down on one knee.

You're not proposing.

You got that right!

Just take a deep breath and come out with it. Just say,

"I love you."

Simple.

So, now what? Well, don't expect her to say, "I love you" back. That isn't why you told her, and besides, having someone tell you that he has fallen in love with you can be something of a shock — she'll probably need a little time to get used to the idea and think about what you've just said.

You hope she feels the same way, but unfortunately it doesn't always work out like that. It's the risk you have to take. Just think — if you never said it, you might never know her true feelings.

Uh-oh.

So, what can you do if the girl of your dreams, who you have just declared your undying love to, turns around and says,

"That's very sweet, but I don't love you."

Not much, I'm afraid.

You've just got to get up, dust yourself off, and accept it. There is no point getting angry, bitter, or aggressive. There is no point trying to win her over with love letters, flowers, or gifts. There is no point trying to force someone to love you.

It doesn't work that way.

The only thing that you can do is accept it and feel sad.

And go back to watching TV!

Falling in love is the best thing that can happen to you.

Surely not as good as winning the Super Bowl?

And it will happen.

There really is someone for everyone, and just about everybody finds someone to fall in love with and be loved by.

So, don't worry — just keep on looking. You'll find someone. It might not be for a while, but almost everyone finds someone to love.

This is a promise?

Getting Intimate

You've gotten past the first date.

Making out!
Getting it on!
Doing the wild thing!

You've gotten past becoming an item with your girlfriend. You've even fallen in love.

Getting intimate is just another dilemma to face.

It's natural: You're with someone who you think is pretty neat, and she thinks you are pretty neat, so you want to explore and touch and cuddle with her.

But it's important that you get intimate with someone for all the right reasons and not all the wrong ones.

So, what are these reasons?

WRONG REASONS:

1. All your friends claim to have done it.
They haven't — guys are terrible braggers. When you all get together, you love to make up stories. You shouldn't, but you do. Almost every guy brags about his conquests, and almost every guy is making it all up. And besides, even if your best friend isn't making it up and has actually undone a girl's bra, that doesn't mean that you have to do the same as him. Take your time.

2. You took a girl to a movie or bought her a pizza.
So you took someone out — it doesn't mean that she owes you. That's just ridiculous. If you think that, you really need to do some serious reconsidering. When a girl gives you a hug, it's because she wants to, not because you bought her a present.

3. You've told a girl that you love her.
Intimacy and love are two different things. It's nice when

they happen together — but they don't always, so don't get one and automatically expect the other.

4. You've been dating for a given length of time.

You can be with someone for years before you both feel ready to commit to any kind of physical love. The whole point about becoming intimate is that everyone has to make his or her own rules. It's much better to wait until you feel the time and the person are right.

> And remember, NO always means NO — it doesn't mean maybe, persuade me, or yes. If you are with someone and you are having a snuggle on the sofa and she wants to stop, YOU'VE GOT TO STOP.
> And likewise, if you want to stop, SHE'S GOT TO STOP.

There is huge pressure on guys to somehow prove that they are real men by getting intimate with as many girls as possible. But you really don't have to if you don't want to. Rather than proving your manhood, this kind of "love 'em and leave 'em" attitude only does one thing: It sends up a giant red flag for girls to stay away from you.

So, What About the Right Reasons?

Well, there is only one really right reason: because you love someone and she loves you.

You want to share something special and be close to someone. Get that right, and a hug will make time stand still.

But you might be tempted to take things further and go to bed with your special someone. For what it's worth, remember it is illegal to have sex if you are under a certain age. The age limit varies from state to state, falling anywhere between fourteen and eighteen years old for straight and gay sex. No, a policeman probably won't break down your bedroom door and arrest you on the spot, but these laws exist for a reason — to protect you.

If you or your girlfriend are thinking about making some sort of physical commitment to each other, the most important thing is not sweet music, low lights, or a romantic setting. The most important thing is to talk, so that you both know what you want.

Getting intimate is great.

It's wonderful, end-of-the-world, lose-yourself-in-someone great.

But if it's not with the right person, or you find yourself going further than you want to and feeling uncomfortable, it can also be lousy. The lousiest thing in the world. So, take your time, decide what's right for you, and make sure your partner knows how you feel.

Safe Sex

If you and your girlfriend have decided you're ready to become intimate, then you should be mature and responsible enough to go about it *safely*. Yes, sex can be wonderful, but there are a lot of things that can go wrong, too.

First of all, as you learned in biology class, the functional reason for sex is to reproduce — in other words, to make babies. Now, if you aren't ready to have a rug rat running around your room while you're doing your homework, be sure that you and your girlfriend take the appropriate precautions — before the fact.

The most common method of pregnancy prevention is to use a condom, otherwise known as a rubber. It's sort of like a one-fingered glove that fits over your penis and catches the semen so it never enters the girl's body. You should be aware, however, that **CONDOMS AREN'T FOOLPROOF** — they *can* break.

Most drugstores sell them, and any package of condoms has detailed instructions about how to put one on. It might not be a bad idea to practice at home, to be sure you know what you're doing before you really need to know. And another thing, you're the one who wears it, so you should be the one who has it on hand. Don't expect your girlfriend to take care of it for you.

Condoms are also crucial in preventing the spread of disease — everything from common sexually transmitted diseases (STD's) like herpes, gonorrhea, and syphilis, which have unpleasant but usually not life-threatening symptoms, to HIV, the AIDS virus, which is deadly and has no known cure.

Now, you may think, "I know my girlfriend. She doesn't have any kind of disease." But what you need to realize is that when you have sex with her, you're also having sex with anyone else she's ever had sex with — at least from a disease standpoint. And since you have no idea what those guys are like, or who they in turn may have had sex with, you can never be too careful.

When you come right down to it, the only no-risk, truly reliable way to avoid pregnancy and disease is not to have sex. But if you feel you're ready, be mature enough to be responsible — to yourself and to your girlfriend.

And if you need more information, take a look at the resources section at the end of this book.

Being Gay

First of all, despite what you might think, **_it isn't weird or abnormal_** to develop huge crushes on, or even be sexually attracted to, members of the same sex. It's just all part of your hormones wreaking havoc during puberty.

It's very common. Does it make you gay? No, it doesn't.

Yeah, well, I've got tons of girls crawling all over me. I just wanted to make that clear!

Sometimes people take crushes a little further and experiment physically with members of the same sex. Again, there is nothing wrong with that. Lots of people experiment with their sexuality.

IN FACT, ONE OUT OF EVERY THREE BOYS AND ONE OUT OF EVERY FIVE GIRLS HAVE FOOLED AROUND WITH MEMBERS OF THE SAME SEX.

Are you freaked out by that?

You shouldn't be. It's completely normal.

Just because you experiment, it doesn't mean that you are gay.

And even if you did decide you prefer other guys to girls, what's the problem with that? It's estimated that one in ten people are gay.

Really?

Just because you might find other guys sexually attractive, it doesn't mean that you are weird, a pervert, or have to start wearing women's underwear.

Gay guys are just the same as straight guys.

They just like other men.

- *They don't watch you in the shower.*
- *They don't try to hit on every guy they talk to.*
- *They don't listen to nothing but Madonna.*
- *They don't cry at the drop of a hat.*
- *They don't all have unhealthy relationships with their mothers.*

Gay men are all around you. They are teachers, rock stars, government officials, lawyers, policemen, comedians, and bus drivers. They live their lives the same as any other guy.

No one should feel isolated or alone because of what he thinks his sexuality might be.

If you think you might be gay because you've got a crush on another guy and

- *you feel isolated, alone, or confused*
- *you think your parents wouldn't understand*
- *you feel that you are the only gay guy in the world*

GO AND TALK TO SOMEONE ABOUT IT.

Oh, yeah, right. Like who?

Your doctor or any of the hot lines listed in the resources section at the end of this book will be able to offer sound advice.

In the same way that finding yourself having a crush on another guy doesn't mean that you *are* gay, dating a girl doesn't necessarily mean that you *aren't* gay.

Some guys have always known that they prefer guys. Some guys try girls and then decide they prefer guys after all. Some guys like both guys and girls (they're bisexual). Some settle down and get married, have children, and then realize that they prefer guys. There are no rules about how you feel or who you should like.

EVERYTHING IS NORMAL.

Always remember that sexuality isn't a switch that is either on or off, gay or straight. It's more like a slide that will eventually nestle somewhere between gay and straight but may be closer to one than the other.

If you have any more questions about this issue, see the resources section at the end of this book.

Breaking Up

Let's start with

Dumping Someone

You might have thought that it was tough getting up the nerve to ask a girl out, making your relationship public, and telling her that you love her. But none of that is as tough as telling her that it's all over.

No one enjoys dumping.

No one likes to see someone upset and sad.

No one likes that look on a girl's face when you are about to tell her that it's all over and she knows what's coming but everything in her eyes is begging you not to say it.

That's a horrible moment.

But sometimes it's the only thing to do.

You can be with someone and love her a lot. She can make you laugh and be your best friend — but if it's time to move on, then it's time to say,

"I'M SORRY — IT'S ALL OVER."

Sometimes things just don't work out.

- *It's nobody's fault.*
- *It's not something that can be avoided.*
- *It just happens.*

A wise man once said that we might not be able to tell the moment when love begins, but we always know the exact moment it ends.

 It wasn't me!

And that is so true.

You can't help falling in love, and you can't help falling out of love. But when you do want to break up, it's best to be honest, face up to your emotions, and respect your soon-to-be ex enough to let her know how you feel.

So, the question is, Is there a right or wrong way to split up with someone? And the answer is, Not really. But there are some basic rules that work when you dump someone, and some things that don't.

> **Golden Dumping Rule:**
> **Be honest and be strong.**

Like Arnold Schwarzenegger.

Telling someone you have been close to that it's all over is never going to be easy. It's a rough ride, and it can be just as bad for the person who is doing the dumping as the person who is being dumped. But no matter how much it hurts you or your girlfriend, when you dump someone, you have to be HONEST. Decide what you want to do and do it. And that's when you have to be STRONG.

It's tough when you are faced with someone who is very upset, someone you care about. It is very tempting to say you're sorry and that you've changed your mind and that you'd like to try to work things out.

But the dumped girl will hate your guts if you tell her it's all over and then let yourself be talked into trying to make it all work out, only to realize after a while that you never wanted to give things a second chance to begin with.

Don't back down.

It's statistically proven that most couples who get to the point of splitting up only to try to make things work out don't succeed. They end up going their separate ways, and there is even more heartache and pain when they finally do break up.

Remember: Decide what you want to do and do it.

Unfortunately, when you break up with someone, it's a time for you to be a little selfish.

Good advice.

If YOU are unhappy in a relationship, YOU have to leave it.

If that means that your girlfriend is going to be upset, cry, and be

heartbroken, that's a real shame — and that should upset you as much as it upsets her. But ultimately it's true that no girl wants to be with a boy if he isn't happy about being with her.

So, by being true to your own feelings, you are doing the right thing by your girlfriend, although she might not see it that way at the time.

It isn't always going to be that easy, and all too often you can find yourself wimping out and making some of the classic all-time dumping mistakes. So, to avoid them, here are a few guidelines for dumping.

Who are you calling a wimp?

1. Where to Dump

Pick the place carefully. Think about it. Striding up to your girlfriend at the mall where she is surrounded by all her friends and saying, **"SORRY BABE—IT'S ALL OVER. I'M GOING OUT WITH YOUR BEST FRIEND,"** and then proceeding to make out with said best friend is pretty mean. Pick a place where you know you can be alone and then tell her, so if she wants to cry and get upset she can (and, equally as important, so can you).

A good place is her house, especially if you know that she is going to be there alone. You'll have somewhere that is private so there can be tears and talk, but it's also somewhere that you can leave when the time comes.

Things can get a little embarrassing if you dump someone at your house and then she refuses to leave until you take it all back.

Oh — I hadn't thought of that. . . .

2. When to Dump

Pick your moment carefully. You owe her that much.

Don't dump her just before she goes on vacation, first thing in the morning at school, or just before exams start.

A good time is a Saturday afternoon — both you and she will have the weekend to start getting over it, and there should be friends around, or at least on the other end of the phone, to lend support.

3. How to Dump

You don't want to do the dumping over the phone, by letter, or in public. That's tacky and shows a lack of respect for the person you are splitting up with. You should always break up with someone to her face — you owe her that — which means you never, ever, ever get a friend to dump someone for you.

Oops!

And don't dump and run. If you are splitting up with someone, you owe her her right to be upset. Listen to

what your girlfriend has to say about splitting up and listen to how she feels about it. You have to face her and her tears. And one of the biggest no-nos is to take the easy way out and start seeing another girl behind your girlfriend's back.

That's pretty cheap and nasty.

Why?

Because you are using that girl to get you out of your relationship with your girlfriend. Your girlfriend is going to be really hurt, and it shows that you just don't care enough to face her and talk things through. If you do leave someone because you've met someone else, that's fine — it happens all the time. But it shows a huge lack of respect for yourself and your current girlfriend if you don't finish one thing before you start another.

Also, it's not fair to make your girlfriend's life so miserable that she dumps you. If you want to get out of the relationship, it's up to you to get out of it. Don't be nasty to her in front of your friends, don't stop phoning her, and don't pretend that she doesn't exist, in the hopes that she'll get the message. That's the coward's way out.

And once you've dumped someone, don't, don't, don't go make out with her next time you're at a party together. Do, and there will be lots of anger and bitterness. And you'll have to go through the whole painful break-up process AGAIN.

4. What to Say

When you do finally tell someone it's all over, **BE TRUTHFUL** about why you want to split up — but don't be nasty.

If there isn't a set reason, you just feel that things aren't working out — say that. That's good enough in itself. Always remember that you are leaving someone because you want to, and never use the line "I'm doing this for your own good,"

Hey, that's one of my best lines!

because you're not, and it's very patronizing.

Oh.

Don't:

- **Say anything hurtful:**

"You were just a phase."

"You're not good enough for me."

"I only went out with you because I felt sorry for you."

- **Say anything condescending:**

"I'll always love you."

"You're too good for me."

"It's not you — it's me."

- **Say anything untrue:**

"This hurts me more than it hurts you."

"I'll never love anyone else."

"No, of course I'm not going out with your best friend."

Do:

- **Be clear and definite:**

> "This really is what I want. I'm sorry if that hurts you, but I think it's for the best."

- **Be kind:**

> "I've had a great time with you and I hope we can stay friends, although I understand you might not want that."

So, that's how to dump — but what if you have *been* dumped?

Getting Dumped

Getting dumped hurts MORE THAN ANYTHING ELSE IN THE WORLD.

You've got that right!

Having your girlfriend turn to you one day and say, "I don't think we should see each other anymore" can make you feel like you've had the rug pulled out from under you, the sky is falling on your head, and you want to curl up into a ball and die.

You have every right to be upset, confused, and sad. But you don't have a right to make your ex's life miserable with phone calls at all hours, unexpected visits, or letters begging for you to get back together.

It's so untrue that if you get dumped by someone you can somehow win them back with flowers, poetry, or persistence. You can't. It's been decided. It's over. It's going to hurt.

It's going to feel like there is nothing you can do to make yourself whole again. You are going to want to see your ex at every opportunity you get — and then hate her every time you do see her. It's a time for you to cry, to mourn the passing of love, to grieve, and then to move on.

IT'S ONE OF THE TOUGHEST TIMES A GUY EVER HAS TO FACE, AND IT'S A TIME FOR COURAGE.

It isn't worth falling in love if you just end up getting hurt — is it?

And don't think that just because you are a guy you aren't allowed to get upset when someone dumps you. Don't think that you have to grin and bear it, take it on the chin, or shrug it off. You are allowed to cry, you are allowed to be upset, and you are allowed to feel like someone has ripped out your still-beating heart and jumped up and down on it. You feel sad — let it all out.

It's the best thing for you, because then you can try to start getting over her. If you don't let out the tears and anger and hurt, then you'll never be able to respect the girl's wishes and respect yourself enough to accept that it really is over.

There is no point trying to deny it, refusing to accept it, or trying to change it. Cry, watch sappy movies, listen to your favorite CDs, do anything to get rid of that gnawing emptiness that you feel inside — because it will go away. It might not feel like it at the time, but it will.

"Gnawing Emptiness" — isn't that a Smashing Pumpkins song?

63

Getting Over It

Dumping and being dumped are the risks we all take when we fall in love, but if we didn't take those risks, we'd never find that special someone, and it's so worth it when you finally find someone who means the world to you.

Still, no one is ever ready to be **HEARTBROKEN**, and no one wants to be a **heartbreaker.**

Fixing a broken heart isn't an easy thing to do. There aren't any instant, just-add-water cures that allow a guy to control his feelings, heal his emotions, and get on with his life.

Hearts don't come with stick-on patches, they can't be fixed with spit and Scotch tape, and no matter how much we try to pretend that everything is fine, it usually isn't.

> **The only thing that will mend a broken heart is time.**

Tick-tock, tick-tock

If you've just been dumped — or if you've just dumped someone — it takes time to get over it. You will probably want to be by yourself a lot, to cry, and to feel blue, which is all fine and normal.

Some days you'll wake up and you'll think that things are hopeless, that you'll never fall in love again, and that you'll be unhappy for the rest of your life.

But it *does* get better.

Slowly, and painfully, hearts heal.

Just don't expect it to happen overnight.

It's a rule of thumb that when someone dumps you, it takes at least as long to get over it as you went out with her for.

You won't be sad for that entire amount of time, and you won't mope around and be depressed. You'll probably date other girls, maybe even have another long-term relationship. But to be totally, completely "I'm fine about this, I really am" over someone can take a **LONG, LONG TIME.** Longer than most people realize.

And don't expect to stop loving someone just because you've been dumped. A broken heart isn't cured by trying to forget that you once really cared for someone, and it isn't about hating them.

When you really and truly fall in love with a girl — no matter what happens — there will always be a part of you that will continue to care for her. That's normal and kind of nice, because it means that you'll never forget that person or the special time you had together.

This is important: You fell in love. It didn't work. You split up.

Don't try to substitute hate for love.

It's always better to remember the good times rather than the bad.

In fact, it will make you happier in the long term.

Really — it will.

And another thing: You don't mend a broken heart by jumping from one girlfriend to another. It's tempting. You feel low; you feel sad; you feel like you want a shoulder to cry on. A lot of guys do it. They split up with a girl, or a girl dumps them, and within days — maybe even hours — they're in another relationship. Unfortunately, it rarely works out.

You can't substitute one emotion for another, and you can't substitute one person for another.

Except in sports.

You've got to give yourself time to get over one relationship before you move on to the next. If you don't give yourself enough time, you'll end up leapfrogging from one unhappy relationship to another, because it's a fact that if you start seeing someone when you are on the rebound, it doesn't last.

I'm on the rebound!

Getting over being in love isn't an exact science. Different things work for different people — but no matter how you go about patching up your heart, dusting yourself off, and finding someone else to love, it's always best to give yourself time.

TiME iS A GREAT HEALER.

Geez, this guy is full of clichés!

Now, before this book turns into a sappy Harlequin romance, let's move on to the next chapter, which talks, among other things, about the old five-fingered shuffle . . . yep, masturbating.

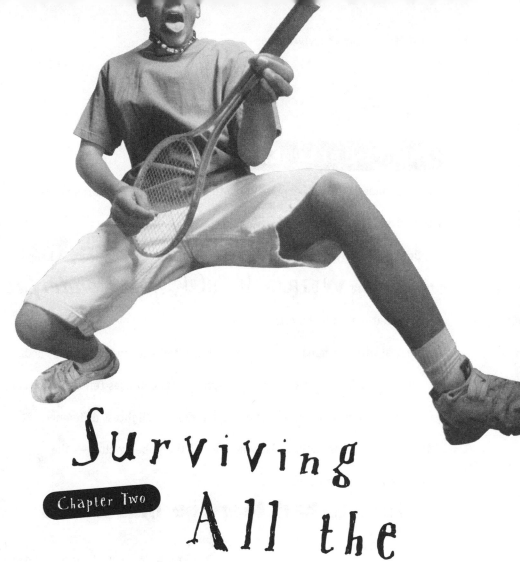

Surviving

Chapter Two

All the
Changes in
Your Body

The Puberty Express

You hit puberty like an express train heading straight for Hormonesville, and all kinds of things begin to happen.

Both your body and mind change, and sometimes it's difficult to keep track of all the **WEIRD**, *wacky*, and *wonderful* things that are happening to you.

We deal with the mind stuff in the next chapter. This one is all about bodies.

Puberty for boys starts and stops anytime between ages ten and eighteen.

It's completely normal, and it doesn't make the slightest difference whether you are an early or late member of the puberty club — the changes will be the same.

Let's kick off with **bad teenage mustaches** (aka facial hair).

What's so bad about that?

Facial Hair

Facial hair starts to grow, but not overnight. Don't expect to go to bed with no hair on your face and wake up the next day looking like Santa Claus.

Ho, ho, ho!

At first, the hair is soft and probably only on your upper lip and maybe on your chin. But over a couple of years, the hair gets thicker and more wiry and spreads all over your cheeks, chin, and upper lip.

And as for when you start to shave — well, that's up to you. However, it's probably best to have at least *something*

Boy — do I need a shave!

there to shave off. If you start to shave too early, you'll only irritate your skin and give yourself a nasty rash.

It's also entirely up to you whether you wet-shave using a razor and shaving cream, or dry-shave with an electric shaver.

Most guys start out wet-shaving because it's quicker and probably easier if you haven't got that much to shave off.

So, what do you need?

WELL, FOR YOUR FIRST SHAVE YOU WILL NEED:

What you need

1. **Some facial hair.** *Duh!*
2. **A razor.**
A disposable one is fine, but one of the more expensive models with a swivel head will give you a more comfortable shave.
3. **Some shaving cream.**
This usually comes in a can, although it is still possible to buy the old-fashioned bars of shaving soap.
4. **A mirror. Obviously.**
5. **Some hot water.**

6. Some moisturizer.

If you don't have any, you could always use some of your mom's or sister's.

My five favorite silly beards: 1. Santa Claus 2. Jazzman goatees 3. Country-and-western-singer beards 4. Merlin and all other wizards 5. Shaggy from Scooby-Doo

AND HOW DO YOU GO ABOUT IT?

1. Run some hot, but not scalding, water and wash your face with normal soap. This softens the bristles and makes them easier to cut.

2. Squirt a small amount of shaving cream into your hand, lather it up, and rub it into your beard. Or lack thereof. The idea with the shaving cream is to reduce the friction between your face and the razor and to soften up the hair even more.

3. Run your razor under some hot water and then begin to shave. Always shave downward and with the growth of the beard. Start with the cheeks and then work over to the upper lip, leaving the chin until last — that's where the toughest hairs grow. Rinse your razor often, either under hot water or in the sink, making sure that the blades aren't becoming clogged with hair.

4. Once you've finished, rinse off any remaining shaving cream with warm water and check for any missed patches. If you've missed a spot, you can run the razor quickly over that particular patch.

I'm as smooth as a baby's bottom (but less smelly).

5. If you're clear, rinse your face with cold water. This helps to close up the pores and seal the skin. Don't splash on tons of aftershave. Aftershave uses alcohol as its base, and that's why when you put it on after shaving, it stings. It's much better to pat your face dry, checking behind the ears for any stray foam, and then use a little moisturizer to give your face back its softness and flexibility.

> **Using moisturizer doesn't make you a wimp.**
> **It's very good for you and protects your skin.**

6. After shaving, it's always best to rinse your razor thoroughly under very hot water, making sure you get rid of any clogged hairs.

7. You should probably change the head of your razor once every two or three shaves — leave it any longer than that and the blades will get dull and won't cut as well. They'll also become a breeding ground for germs and bacteria. Not nice.

Eeeeww!

8. If you cut yourself while shaving, don't stick on a little bit of toilet paper. That will do nothing for you, and as soon as you take the paper off, you'll start to bleed again. It's better to let the skin close up on its own. Now, if you suffer from particularly bad zits or acne, then shaving can be something of a **nightmare.**

 Ouch!

If it's just the occasional eruption, you can probably steer your razor around it, but if you are suffering from a really bad attack, you can try one of two things:

1. Grow a beard.

(Which is not only not allowed in some schools but also makes you look like a cowboy — fine in the wild West, *Yee-less* fine in New Jersey.) or *haw!*

2. Use an electric razor.

Why? Well, if you dry-shave with an electric shaver, your skin won't be irritated by the use of shaving cream. A decent electric razor can be bought for about forty bucks and will be gentler on the skin.

If you want to try using one, it's probably best to go for a multiheaded razor with three small metal foils that make a triangle on the shaving face.

The other main type of electric razor has one single, long foil.

This is fine, too, but the three-headed version gives you more control over a bumpy surface.

Just like with a wet razor, you have to clean the shaving heads after every shave to stop the buildup of hair, skin, and bacteria.

Which brings us to:

Pimples, Zits, Eruptions

(Otherwise known as acne.)

Almost everybody gets the occasional zit during puberty — but unfortunately, some people get them worse than others. What can you do?

Unfortunately, very little.

Zits are caused by pores in your skin becoming blocked by excess oils . . . that have been released because of the **hormone riot** going on in your body . . . that in turn has been caused by puberty.

And you don't just get them on your face. They can also appear on your back and shoulders and, to a lesser extent, on your chest.

So what can be done about these **PESKY, RED, PUS-FILLED monsters?**

The most important thing is to wash regularly with an unscented soap. You can try using a medicated soap or one of the many anti-zit creams and applications that you can buy at the drugstore, but they will probably do little good.

Normal soap and water are just as effective as any scientifically tested, new-and-improved breakthrough.

If your zits get particularly bad, you should see your doctor, who can prescribe drugs to reduce the redness and swelling.

The two most important things to remember about zits are that:

- *You should try to not feel depressed about them. They usually go away eventually and leave you with a smooth complexion.*
- *You shouldn't* Scratch, **PICK**, *or* **POP** *them.* *The temptation can be almost overwhelming to squeeze those zits. But don't. If you do, you might end up with scarring.*

Greasy Hair

The same greasiness and excess oils that cause zits can also give you particularly greasy hair. Again, wash your hair often and thoroughly, and you should be able to keep the gloopiness down to a minimum.

Don't forget that during puberty, while your body is changing, your hormones will be in **FULL-ON PARTY MODE.** That's why you get zits and greasy hair.

And that's also why you will, to be frank, begin to smell.

How come I never get invited to hormone parties?

Being Stinky

It's perfectly normal — your glands are growing and changing, and for a while they will produce particularly strong-smelling sweat. It's nothing to be ashamed of — but it is a good idea to get under the shower or into a hot bath and have a good scrubdown *regularly*.

But girls like that manly smell!

You are going to get especially smelly under your arms and around your penis and scrotum and on your feet.

So wash them.

Every day.

And don't forget to change your shirt.

There is no point getting yourself smelling sweet as a daisy only to put a stinky shirt back on.

Don't know how to clean a shirt?

It's very simple.

1. Put the shirt and some laundry detergent in the washing machine and turn it on.
2. Dry the shirt.
2a. Iron the shirt (optional).
3. Wear the clean shirt.

Notice that at no point in that list are the words "Wait for Mom, Dad, or anyone else to wash the shirt for you." *But it's a little-known fact that after six months they stop smelling!*

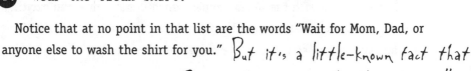

75

There is nothing worse than body odor, or **B.O.**, but sometimes it just can't be helped. All you can do is shower or bathe every day and use a good, strong deodorant.

Whether you use a spray, stick, or roll-on deodorant is up to you, but if you use a spray, it's less likely to block the pores under your arms and cause an infection — something that can happen with roll-ons and sticks.

You can also use an aftershave and splash it all over your body to help hide any smells.

> *But aftershave isn't a substitute for washing, and remember that a little goes a long way.*

A quick splash on your chest will cover up a multitude of nasty aromas that might develop after you've had a good wash with plenty of hot water and soap. But too much will make you smell like the perfume counter at Macy's, which is just as bad.

So, what about the other changes that happen to your body during puberty?

Voices

How come you can be talking to someone and have a shrill voice one second and then after a bit of a **WoBbLe,** a deep, booming voice the next?

Well, it has to do with the Adam's apple, which is not a new and exciting form of fruit, but the part of your body that's just below your chin, sticks out a bit, and hurts like hell if you ever get punched on it.

Its job is to be in charge of the change in a guy's voice.

If you get a little excited when your voice first starts to break, it will all of a sudden sound like you've been sucking a helium balloon. This is nothing to worry about. It will settle down given a little time and find its natural, deeper pitch.

How **L O N G** will it take?

Well, that's impossible to say. For some guys, your voice can take months to break completely; for others it can happen over a couple of weeks.

Body Hair

I'm afraid if you think you're going to go from smoothly smooth to a walking carpet in a matter of days, then you've got another think coming.

It's perfectly normal for body hair to develop at different times on different parts of your body, so if you've got hairy legs, don't expect to have a chest rug at the same time.

> It's weird, but some guys really are hairier than others.

Like Bigfoot. Now, that's hairy!

But don't think that just because you've got a little bit more chest hair, it makes you more of a man — it doesn't.

And despite what you might have heard, it's not unusual to have hairs growing on your back and on your butt cheeks.

A hairy butt! Well, guess it keeps you from getting cold!

77

Some girls make a big thing about not liking hairy backs and butts.

BUT **DON'T WORRY ABOUT IT.**

Unless you look in a mirror, you're not going to be able to see them, and if a girl gets to the stage where she sees your back or your butt, hopefully she'll have other things on her mind.

You'll also notice hair in that whole area below the belt. A mass of thick, wiry hairs, called pubic hair or pubes, starts to grow.

Again, no two guys are exactly the same, so if you are in the shower after football practice and you cast a quick eye around at the pride and joy of the varsity squad, you are going to see different sizes and shapes of penises and different amounts of pubic hair.

And by the way, you don't need to cut pubic hair. It reaches a certain length and then stops. You don't need to pop down to the local barber and ask for a bit off the top and a genital trim. But if you do have to shave your pubes, maybe because of an operation, they *will* grow back. They're clever like that.

 Just a trim please – and watch what you're cutting!

So, let's get down to your:

Plumbing

Otherwise known as your *family jewels,* your **pride and joy,** your **PACKAGE,** your genitals.

 Does your mom know you're saying this?

Boys have the bodily equivalent of the Bermuda Triangle, which covers the entire area of their genitals. And all through puberty, things seem to appear and disappear in this area for what seems like no reason at all, although hopefully no ships or planes will go missing inside your boxers.

So, what actually happens?

For one thing, a boy's testicles and penis get bigger.

How big?

Well, how long is a piece of string?

It varies, but not as much as you might think. Before puberty, a boy's penis is about one to two inches long when soft. After puberty, it's about two to four inches when soft and five to six inches when hard.

Now, before all you guys go running off to find a ruler, no two guys are the same.

OK — but do you have a ruler I could borrow later?

And *size makes no difference*

as to how well it works.

And if you are wondering whether the way you hang is the same as the way every other guy hangs, it is, more or less. You'd be surprised just how similar all penises are. Sure, no two are the *same*, but they all follow the same *basic design*.

Does it have a trademark?

79

Yours might curve off to the side a little or even curve up a little. THAT'S PERFECTLY NORMAL. Some guys have circumcised penises, which means that they have had an operation at some point in their lives to permanently pull back their foreskin, the piece of soft skin that covers the head of your penis. It doesn't affect the way it works or what it feels like to be the proud owner of one.

And some guys have only one testicle instead of the more usual two. They're either born that way or have had one removed for medical reasons. If you only have one ball, it doesn't affect how it works, what it feels like, or whether you will be able to become a dad.

I wonder if anyone has ever had three?

So most penis and testicle sets are more or less the same, and they all do the same things.

When you hit puberty, all of a sudden things in the pants department start doing stuff all by themselves.

Like what? Practicing the piano, taking out the garbage, doing my chemistry homework — now, that would be useful!

You can be waiting for the bus or standing in the lunch line and all of a sudden . . . **HELLO!**

And as for first thing in the morning, well, not all guys join the Scouts — but when they wake up, all guys can make a tent with their natural equipment and the bedspread.

A what? . . . Oh, I get it!

We are talking **erections,** HARD-ONS, BONERS. They come and go without any rhyme or reason. **But don't panic.**

Just because you get a hard-on in public doesn't mean that everyone can see. Only Superman has X-ray vision. It might feel like it's sticking out like a flagpole, it might feel like you can't walk or that you've got an extra leg, but it isn't that noticeable.

So, now that you've got this thing looking up at you at every turn, what are you going to do with it?

You want to explore it. You want to poke and prod it, to — let's be frank — masturbate.

Masturbation

Otherwise known as **jerking off, pulling the plowman, DOING THE FIVE-FINGER SHUFFLE,** *pulling the pickle,* SPANKING THE MONKEY, self-service, and CHOKING THE CHICKEN . . . to name but a few.

Should we be talking about this?

Some people think masturbation is a dirty thing to do — but it isn't, and despite what you might have heard, everyone does it.

Everyone.

And you know what? There is nothing wrong with it. It's fun and it feels nice. Otherwise people wouldn't be doing it in the first place.

So, let's clear up a few of the stupid myths that surround masturbation.

I'm glad all this is true — otherwise I'd be in real trouble!

- **It won't make you go crazy or blind.**
- **It won't make hair grow on your palms.**
- **It won't make your penis fall off.**
- **It won't give you zits.**
- **It won't make you infertile.**
- **It won't make you a pervert.**
- **It won't affect your ability to have sex in the future.**

Now, it's sometimes thought that masturbation is wrong or a sin, which is fine if that's what some people want to think, but always remember:

> **It's what you think and feel that matters.**

Whew!

Never let anyone make you feel guilty for doing something that is perfectly natural.

What every sex expert agrees is that masturbation is the best way to discover things about your body and how you like to be touched. It's a way of exploring and discovering things about yourself, and

there is **absolutely** nothing wrong with it.

Masturbating once, twice, even three times a month, a week, a day, an hour . . . that's all perfectly natural and perfectly fine.

As a very great man once said, nobody should knock masturbation — after all, it's sex with someone you love.

Woody Allen said that!

Masturbation

OK, so it's normal. Everyone does it.

But what do you actually **do?**

Well, the dictionary definition of masturbation is the stimulation of the genitals by oneself until one reaches a sexual climax.

Huh?

In plain English that means you touch and stroke your penis, usually back and forth and up and down, until a warm, tingly sensation starts building around your penis, and you begin to stroke faster and faster.

You might start thinking sexy thoughts about girls, your geography teacher, or a favorite rock star. The **tingly sensation** grows and spreads around your body until it reaches a climax that almost hurts. But it's a nice type of hurt, like a big sneeze.

Achoooooo!

That's when you "come" and white sticky stuff, your semen, spurts out of the end of your penis. And **it feels really nice.**

That's masturbating. And one very, very important point: You never, ever run out of semen. You could masturbate every day, all day, for hours on end, and all you would end up with is a tired wrist and a sore penis. No guy has got a limited supply of semen — your testicles make it on demand. Don't worry — you won't run out.

It's not just masturbating that involves you, your best friend, and a sticky mess.

You might also have . . .

Wet Dreams

What's a wet dream?

Well, it's a dream, usually — but not always — about sex that results in a boy having an orgasm in his sleep. You wake up in the morning and find a sticky spot on your sheets. There is nothing to be embarrassed about. Everyone has had one, and you couldn't stop yourself even if you wanted to, because it's your body doing what's natural.

Guys grow out of wet dreams — but no one ever grows out of masturbation. Ever.

So, these are your body changes and what you can expect from them.

Remember: If in doubt, trust to nature. Your body knows what it's doing, even if you don't.

Sexy Thoughts

While you are exploring your plumbing, you might think sexy thoughts. That's fine, too — it's called FANTASIZING, and everyone does it.

Just because you might have sexy thoughts about your math teacher dressed as a large rabbit jumping up and down on a trampoline doesn't mean that you want it to happen. When you have sexy thoughts, you are just imagining things; you don't necessarily want them to actually happen.

You should **NEVER FEEL GUILTY** about what you think about when you masturbate. Whatever it is, it's normal — just don't expect it to come true.

Please, not my math teacher. Yuck!

Magazines

Now, you might get a little tired of just *thinking* about girls and want to start *looking* at some instead — some with few or no clothes on. You might start getting distracted by magazines every time you go to your local newsstand — either fashion magazines that have girls dressed in see-through tops or maybe the ones on the top shelf. You know — the ones with titles like *Voluptuous Vixens,* **Sexy Singles,** and **Big and Bouncy.**

Hey, that's my favorite!

You might even want to buy one, but it's against the law to sell you a porn magazine if you are under eighteen.

Just because you get your hands on a copy of *Nude Girls in Jell-O*, or sneak a peek at the underwear section of your mom's mail order catalog, it doesn't make you a pervert. Hundreds of thousands of men and even some women regularly buy and enjoy pornography. After all, porn has been around for thousands of years.

If you think that the contents of girly magazines are a bit shocking, you should see some ancient Roman mosaics and statues. Now, *they* would make your eyes pop out.

Where would I see these mosaics again?

But if you have found a copy of *Big and Bouncy* and are reading it at home, there are some important things to remember.

Models in general, and models in pornography in particular, aren't average women.

They're probably taller, slimmer, and have bigger breasts than anyone else you know. And the same goes for movie stars and rock stars. They are glamorous, beautiful, and sexy. That's part of why they do what they do — because their bodies are considered to be either perfect or sexy.

So don't expect your girlfriend to measure up to the girl on the centerfold. For one thing, your girlfriend won't have a staple through her belly.

Unless she's got a pierced belly button!

All pictures in magazines have been posed, and the women have been heavily made up to look sexy, and possibly had plastic surgery to enhance their breasts and/or facial features. In addition, the photographs have usually been touched up and enhanced before they're printed.

Never forget that pornography isn't real — **it's fantasy.**

The porn industry is one of the biggest in the world, making more money each year than all the Hollywood blockbusters put together, which means there are a lot of people using pornography, not just you.

Don't feel guilty.

Just because you got a copy of a girly magazine and used it to masturbate with, you are not a pervert. You're still going to be able to get it on with your girlfriend, and you won't turn into a rapist.

Some people feel that any form of pornography is exploitation, and that the women in the magazines and films are being used and abused purely for the pleasure and gratification of men.

Whether you use pornography is a completely personal decision. If you think or feel that it's exploitation, and wrong, then there are no rules that say you have to use it.

But what do you do if your mom finds your copy of *Big and Bouncy?*

Shrivel up and die?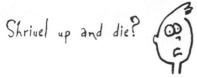

One thing is almost certain — she is not going to be happy. It might be that part of the fun of having a girly magazine in your room is that you have to hide it from prying eyes. It makes it all the more exciting because it isn't allowed.

However, that doesn't change the fact that if it is finally found, the sparks will probably fly.

So, what can you expect?

Well, everyone is different and everyone's mom is different. Some moms might **ignore it,** some might choose just to **THROW IT OUT,** some moms will want to talk about it, and some moms will **Go BALLiSTiC.**

All these reactions, and any in between, are understandable. After all, you brought a porno magazine into your parents' house, and they might not like that.

It's always best to remember three things when it comes to moms and magazines with pictures of women with no clothes on:

1. Your mom is a woman, *No, really?*
and a lot of women find any form of pornography highly
objectionable.

2. Your mom is older than you, and she might have different views about what is acceptable. What you feel is fine,
she might find obscene.

3. Your mom may still think of you as her "little boy,"
and it might be a surprise to her that you are having
sexual feelings now.

A WORD OF WARNING

Looking at a magazine full of naked or beautiful women is easy. It's a lot easier than talking to a real girl, flirting with her, asking her out, and trying to form a long-term relationship with her.

When you use porn, there is no fear of rejection, no fear of being hurt — you just open the cover and you've got an instant two-dimensional girlfriend.

I prefer my girls to be flesh and blood! They are more squeezable!

But sometimes people replace real relationships with real girls with a fantasy relationship with the perfect women in the magazines. Don't let it happen. Your interests might be getting out of proportion if:

- *you ever find your mattress is getting so lumpy that you can't sleep on it because of your vast stash of girly magazines or*
- *you find yourself more interested in spending every evening in your*

bedroom with **Big and Bouncy** *than going out with your friends.*

So? What's wrong with that?

Looking at the occasional porn magazine is natural and fine. Almost every guy has bought something that could be described as porn at some point in his life.

YOU'RE NOT WEIRD BECAUSE YOU'VE JOINED THE CLUB.

But if it gets to the point where you have tons and tons of these things hidden away, then you might want to talk to someone about why you prefer to look at nudey pictures rather than talk to real girls.

I only read the articles!

Maybe you wouldn't feel comfortable talking to your mom or dad, but a brother or your doctor could help.

> *Real girls are much better: They're people.*
> *They talk. They have opinions. And they laugh.*

They're soft and cuddly, and you can go on dates with them. When was the last time you saw a guy taking his copy of *Big and Bouncy* for a hot date at McDonald's?

Well, actually, there is this one really weird guy....

Surviving

Chapter Three

Teenage

Ups and

Downs

Emotions

Guys have them. They might not like to think that they do — but they do. They feel **HAPPY**, sad, **LONELY**, **ANGRY**, **BITTER**, and jealous in the same way that everyone else does.

But the thing with guys is that they just aren't very good at expressing all these emotions. They tend to bottle them up, push them down, and try to ignore them. Society as a whole teaches guys to be this way — to "stay in control" rather than "let it all out."

That's all right for girls — they can get together with a few friends, watch a three-hankie movie, share some secrets, and have a cry and a hug.

Guys don't do that.

Can you imagine calling up your best friend and saying, "I feel so sad, I want to cry. Will you hug me?"

Ha, ha — who would ever say that??

It isn't going to happen.

Still, guys need to find healthy outlets for their emotions. They need to understand their feelings in order to work through them. And the first step to understanding emotions is recognizing them.

What Is Depression?

Depression can mean just feeling sad and low for a couple of days, or in more serious cases, it can be a medical condition that needs treatment with either counseling or prescribed drugs.

SO, HOW CAN YOU TELL IF YOU ARE DEPRESSED?

You feel sad and listless, with little or no energy.

You might think that there isn't any point doing anything, and you might feel isolated and alone. There is nothing wrong with feeling that way for a week or so — sometimes that's what being a teenager is like. But if those feelings go on longer or you feel down for a couple of weeks, happy for a couple of days, and then down again, it's probably worth seeing your doctor about it.

Like a seesaw.

Why Teenagers Have Ups and Downs

Anyone can become depressed, no matter what their age. You can be seventy or seventeen and feel blue.

It's a myth that teenagers don't get depressed.

They do.

One in eight teenagers suffers from depression.

Many of them are guys.

Depression can be caused by almost anything, and often there seem to be no reasons at all. A lot of teenagers get depressed because of:

1. Puberty

Again!

One of the main reasons that teenagers in particular can have **mood swings** and feel sad has to do with the hormone party that is puberty.

Well, at least someone is having a good time.

Puberty is a very unsettling time when your body goes through massive changes. Your hormones are at the center of it, wreaking havoc inside your body.

And the hormones don't just affect you physically. They affect you emotionally, too, with the result that you can go from feeling fine to feeling like the sky is about to fall on you in a matter of minutes.

But hang in there, because although you can still get depressed after puberty, once your hormones have begun to settle down, the sad feelings will begin to lessen.

It's a Bummer!

Phew!

2. Other Reasons

Everybody is bound to get depressed if certain things happen. For instance:

- *your girlfriend dumps you*
- *your parents split up*
- *you have an argument with your best friend*
- *you have to change schools*
- *someone close to you dies.*

These things are upsetting and always take time to get over.

If You're Feeling Down

So, what can you do if things aren't going so great?

If you are **sad,** you have to let it all out.

Bottle up feelings and you'll become an emotional pressure cooker ready to explode in a big, sticky mess. According to doctors, if you bottle up emotions and deny them a release, you can make yourself physically ill. It's just not worth it. So, how can you release them?

1. Cry.

What is it with boys and crying? We don't want to look like girls.

If you feel unhappy and you have a good cry, it doesn't make you less of a man. It doesn't make you a big sissy or somehow weak. Guys <u>are</u> allowed to be upset and vulnerable.

If you think being a real man is all about grinning and bearing it, you're wrong. Truly being a real man is all about understanding your emotions and giving them free rein.

Been dumped? Start crying.

Your team out of the Stanley Cup finals? *That will always make me cry!*

Start crying.

Someone close to you died? Start crying.

Just feel down in the dumps? Start crying.

I GUARANTEE THAT IT'LL MAKE YOU FEEL BETTER.

2. Exercise.

Sometimes, if you feel depressed, all you want to do is spend the whole day in bed or in your room with the curtains closed and dark and **MOODY** music playing.

However, it's been proven that one of the best things for depression is plenty of exercise and a good diet. If you spend all day in bed because you feel sad, you are more likely to feel sadder, not happier.

Feel a little low?

Go and run around the block a few times or *shoot some hoops.*

You'll probably feel a lot better, and the exercise will do you good.

3. Talk.

It's really tough to talk about your emotions, but it's the best thing in the world if you feel sad and you just can't seem to stop yourself from feeling that way. You might be surprised, but just the act of talking to someone about a problem — even if they don't say anything back to you — often helps. For one thing, it helps you think the problem through by putting words to your feelings.

Just getting it off your chest, unloading, and then taking a deep breath and getting on with the rest of your life is a great thing to do, and it will make you feel so much better.

4. See a doctor.

If your depression won't go away, it may be serious. Counseling and/or medication can help. A visit to a school counselor or psychiatrist will help determine if your depression is medically based and needs to be treated.

If you don't know where to go for help, see the resources section at the back of this book.

> *Golden Depression Rule: Never think you are alone. Talk to people.*

Always remember:

- *Just because you are a guy doesn't mean that you have to bury your feelings way down inside.*
- *Just because you are a guy doesn't mean that you aren't allowed to feel sad and angry.*
- *Just because you are a guy doesn't mean that you aren't allowed to cry, to break down and sob your heart out.*

Confidence

BELIEVING IN YOURSELF enough to put your ideas across, to stand up and make yourself heard, or just to believe in what you want to do can be a tough thing to master.

Everyone goes through periods of not being confident, of doubting their abilities, or just doubting themselves in general.

But unless you get on top of it, this lack of confidence can really ruin your life, because you'll find yourself missing out on so much.

Feeling:

- **shy,**
- **nervous around people,**
- **inadequate,**
- **insecure,** or
- **unimportant**

is a sign of a lack of confidence, and they are more common than you might think.

Building Your Confidence

What can you do to build up your self-confidence?
You could start with a list. **What if I can't write?**

It's not dorky, it's not silly, and no one ever has to know.

On one side of a piece of paper, write down a list of the things about your personality that you might not like.

They might be:

- *I'm shy.*
- *I'm not very good at speaking in class.*
- *I get embarrassed.*
- *I blush a lot.*
- *I'm jealous of my older brother.*

Enough already!

You'll probably find it's pretty easy to come up with a longish list.

That's not unusual — most people find it easier to come up with their bad qualities rather than their good ones.

Now, beside your list of things you don't like, write down the things about yourself that you do like, to cancel out the bad stuff.

Write down one $good$ thing for every **BAD** thing that you've listed.

They might be:

- *I'm funny.*
- *I'm smart.*
- *I'm nice.*

This list will probably be tougher. Coming up with a long list of good things about yourself can be a real challenge.

Don't worry. It doesn't mean that there aren't good things to find out about you — it just means that you'll probably have to look harder and dig a little deeper.

If you are really having trouble coming up with enough, there is nothing wrong with asking your family what your good points are. You don't have to tell them that you are making a list — just ask them.

Dig a little deeper.

So you've got two lists of qualities, one next to the other — some good,

some not so good. Yup.   Yup.

Now get the biggest, thickest, blackest marker you can find and cross out each bad point one at a time.

Really scrub them out.

Go at it like there's no tomorrow.

Get rid of them, so you can't see any of these things that you don't like about yourself.

Once you've done that, you will be left with a list of

good things.

Positive things.

EXCELLENT THINGS about yourself.

I get it!

Fold up this list of your great qualities and put it in your pocket or in your wallet. Every time you feel lacking in confidence, pull out the list and read through all your good points.

It might sound silly. It might sound weird.

BUT IT REALLY WORKS.

It's just a way or reminding yourself that you are a pretty neat person even if you don't feel it.

If you worry about expressing your ideas because you think that everyone will laugh, just take a second and think: If someone else suggested this idea, would I laugh?

If the answer is no, then why should anybody laugh at you if you make the same suggestion?

If you worry about public speaking: Practice.

Sit up in your room, close the door, and talk out loud.

Talk to yourself.

Who, me?

Read the sports page. Say anything that you want.

Because what you'll be doing is getting used to the sound of your own voice.

Most people don't really know what they sound like when they talk loudly in a quiet room. You sound different, and it can be quite a surprise. If you've got a speech to make, an oral report, or an interview fast approaching, there is nothing wrong with practicing a bit ahead of time.

Have to deliver a speech to the rest of your class?

Read through it out loud a couple of times beforehand. Get used to hearing your own voice say those words.

Again, you might think that this all sounds a bit weird.

BUT IT WORKS.

Before you go into an interview or before you leave for a party or before you stand up in class to give a report, there is nothing wrong with taking a deep breath and very quickly saying to yourself:

I'm great.

I'm good.

I'm pretty amazing.

I can do this.

I know what I'm talking about.

And everyone is going to be interested.

OK, OK —
I'm great,
I'm wonderful,
blah, blah,
blah, blah.

It will help to build your confidence at the moment you need it the most.

Body Language

Confidence isn't just about what you say with your mouth. It's also about what you say with your body. Body language will express as much as what you say.

Pop Quiz

If you've got to meet someone important for the first time and you are going to be expected to shake his or her hand, which of these is better?

A. Stand up straight, with your shoulders back and your head held high. Grasp his or her hand firmly when you shake it and look him or her in the eye when you say hello.

B. Shuffle in, slumped over and talking to the floor. Give him or her a limp handshake and mumble a hello over his or her shoulder.

The answer is A, of course.

You can use positive body language at parties, too.

Here's a little secret: Ask any girl what she finds attractive in a guy, and she will list a few things: **SENSE OF HUMOR, nice butt,** and CONFIDENCE.

If you are going to a party, remember that you've been invited because you are interesting and that someone wants you to be there.

When you talk to someone, look them in the eyes, listen to what they are saying, and you'll get along like a house on fire.

Stand-up comedians say that 95% of the trick in telling jokes, performing in front of a crowd, and being funny is confidence. If you are confident (or *seem to be* confident), people will pick up on that and you'll be a big hit.

Have you heard the one about...

But what can you do if you get criticized even after all this practicing?

Coping with Criticism

If you do some homework and get a bad grade, if you tell a joke at lunchtime and no one laughs, or if you try to explain something and it comes out all wrong, your confidence can suffer a real setback.

Nothing is more likely to knock someone's confidence than criticism.

No one likes being criticized. However, criticism can be very useful. It can help guide you in your work and teach you when some actions are more appropriate than others.

Good criticism isn't about pulling apart something you've done — it's about highlighting strong points as well as weaknesses.

If someone criticizes you heavily, all you can do is walk away and think about it.

• Ask yourself why *the person is criticizing you*.

Sometimes people use the chance to criticize to deliberately put someone down and make them feel insecure. It could be that they are jealous of you or very INSECURE about themselves. It's a **POWER GAME** *that some people like to play, and you only let them win if you let their criticism affect you. You shouldn't. However, bear in mind that someone might actually be trying to help you, in which case:*

• Ask yourself if the criticism is right.

A lot of criticism is based on opinion. Someone has disagreed with what you've said or done. If that person is important to you and you trust his or her judgment, then it might be worth thinking about whether the criticism is justified. If it is not and you think what you've done is right and worthwhile, don't take any notice of him or her.

• Ask yourself if the criticism is really criticism at all.

Sometimes you might be feeling paranoid and take something someone says as a criticism, even when it isn't meant to be. Like what? Well, say your mom says, "Do you really like this music?" You might mistake that for criticism of your taste when in fact it is only a question.

Paranoid? I'm not paranoid! It's the others — all out to get me — I know they are. Paranoid? Not me!

Whatever you want to say or do, you shouldn't ever let your own lack of confidence get in the way.

Practice,

take your time,

think about what you've got to do.

CONFIDENCE CAN BE LEARNED.

After all, we all have something to say. It is just a matter of finding our own voice.

Unfortunately, a lot of guys have trouble with a lack of confidence, and instead of reading brilliant books like this one to find out how to make themselves more confident, they depend on tricks to cover up their lack of confidence.

Which brings us neatly to the next chapter. . . .

Chapter Four

Surviving Teenage Social Life

Peer Pressure

Is that like tire pressure?

When guys get together, they sometimes do silly things.

IT'S ALL PART OF BEING A GUY.

They egg each other on because they think they're being cool.

They think whatever they are doing is going to impress the girls, or

THEY JUST WANT TO LOOK TOUGH.

Here are some of the things guys do when they get together:

- *Make mean jokes about girls or gays,*
- *bully,*
- *skip school,*
- *drink,*
- *take drugs,*
- *fight,* and
- *brag about the number of girls they've been with.*

You might think these things make you look cool in the eyes of your

friends or girls, but instead, they almost always:

- *make you look stupid,*
- *make you feel really ill, or even*
- *do long-term damage to your body.*

D'oh!

So is it worth it? **NO .**

Will guys still do them?

Probably.

Unfortunately, that's what guys can be like when they get together —
kind of stupid.

But **you** don't have to be.

Saying No

It's difficult not to succumb to peer pressure. If everyone else is
doing something, it's hard to say no.

You might think you are going to be called a *sissy*, **a party
pooper,** or a *coward.* It takes a lot of courage and self-control to
say no to your friends and people to whom you want to seem cool.

You'd rather stay in with your girlfriend than go to the movies with your
friends? It can be difficult to say no, but if that's what you want to do,
then you should.

You don't want to shoplift, even though all your friends are doing it,
because you know it's **DUMB**, **risky,** and **WRONG?**
It takes real guts to walk away from them. But think about it this way:
If these people really are your friends and you really don't want to do
something, then they should respect that. If they don't, and they call you
names, then they probably aren't such great friends.

It's particularly important
when it comes to things which
can actually hurt you:

> *Always remember:*
> *Do what you want to do.*
> *Don't, and you'll regret it.*

Substances That Make You Feel Great... or Not So Great

Booze

You might go to a party with the belief that if you have a drink, you will automatically seem more *charming,* **ATTRACTIVE,** and funny to all the girls in the room. You won't.

If I became any more charming, attractive, or funny, I'd have to carry a government health warning.

Sooner or later, a lot of guys end up passed out in the bathroom with vomit all over their shirts and feeling like death warmed over. And then, after you have stumbled home, gone straight to bed, probably throwing up at least once more on the way, there is the next morning.

YOU WAKE UP FEELING AWFUL.

YOUR HEAD HURTS.

Your **stomach** hurts.

Sounds like fun ... NOT!

Your arms and legs hurt.

EVERYTHING HURTS.

And then you remember what you did.

- *You remember trying to put your hand up the shirt of that really cute girl from your math class.*
- *You remember crushing beer cans with your head.*
- *You remember drop-kicking the cat across the yard.*

You look in the mirror and say to yourself, **"I'll never drink again."**

Why? Why do we put ourselves through it?

Again, it mainly comes down to peer pressure.

If all your friends are drinking, then it must be something that real guys do.

Booze

 Uh-oh.

First of all, it's illegal to buy or consume alcohol if you are under twenty-one, so drinking shouldn't even be an issue to begin with. However, in the real world, things usually aren't that cut-and-dried — teenagers have parties, and more often than not, they've found a way to have alcohol there.

But that doesn't change the fact that teenage drinking is illegal and can carry some hefty consequences. Possession of alcohol as a minor could get you detention in a Department of Youth Services facility and probation. But that's not even the worst-case scenario. Eight youths a day die in alcohol-related car accidents. In fact, more than 40% of all sixteen- to twenty-year-old deaths result from car crashes, and about half of these accidents are alcohol-related. Is it all really worth it for a few hours of "fun"?

So, what's a guy to do? You don't want to miss out on all the parties (especially since that girl from math class is sure to be there), but if you do go, chances are there'll be people drinking, as well as the pressure to join in.

Is it only a choice of too much or nothing at all when it comes to booze? Well, legal issues aside, no. It is possible to avoid feeling left out of the party without getting blotto and acting like a jerk. The problem, though, is that **alcohol affects your brain.**
It relaxes you,
makes you feel more free and easy.
It gives you self-confidence —
it makes you feel funny and popular. It makes you burp, too.

It also affects your judgment, so the more you drink, the less likely you are to be able to judge when you've had enough. Which means you are likely to drink more, because you think you can handle it. Which will affect your judgment. Which means you are likely to drink more, because you think you can handle it. Which will affect your judgment. Which means you are likely to drink more, because you think you can handle it. Which will affect your judgment. Which means you are likely to drink more, because you think you can handle it. Which will affect your judgment. Which means you are likely to drink more, because you think you can handle it. Which will affect your judgment.

And so on and so on.

But surely that isn't such a bad thing if it makes it easier for you to talk to people and makes you feel more relaxed or makes you funnier?

Not true.

The weird thing about booze is that it makes you *think* you are being **FUNNY**, *charming*, and **POPULAR**, but you probably aren't. You're probably just being **LOUD**, **NOISY**, and **obnoxious**.

> **Alcohol doesn't change the people we are inside.**

Alcohol is not a magic potion that will turn an unhappy and insecure person into a happy and popular one. In fact, different people are affected by alcohol in different ways. Some people just become very giggly and a little silly. Others become angry and aggressive.

And never forget that if you drink excessively, you are setting yourself up for all kinds of medical problems.

Like?

1. Hangovers

You have the fun — you pay the price. **HANGOVERS HURT!** they make you feel awful for days after your drinking spree. They affect your ability to think straight and work properly. You feel *tired*, because when you are drunk, you don't sleep properly. Your stomach will feel awful and you might **THROW UP**, because alcohol in large quantities irritates the stomach lining, and your head will hurt because you, quite simply, poisoned yourself.

2. Alcohol Poisoning

If you drink too much booze at one time, you can **POISON** yourself. The body processes alcohol by absorbing it into the bloodstream and then passing it through the body — that's how it gets to your brain and makes you feel tipsy. However, if you overload the bloodstream with more alcohol than it can cope with, it reaches toxic levels. Then it could be off to the hospital to have your stomach pumped in order to get rid of any remaining alcohol there before it has a chance to get into the bloodstream. Not fun.

Don't forget about beer bellies!

3. Liver Damage

Drink too much for too many years, and you will set yourself up for a whole load of problems in later life. Liver damage, also known as cirrhosis, is an illness directly linked with drinking. The liver is the organ in the body that cleans the blood. It's your built-in filter. If you pass too much alcohol through it over a period of years, it will just pack up and stop working. And then you are in **REAL TROUBLE.**

This is all very cheerful!

4. Strokes

Strokes are caused by hemorrhages in your brain. Blood leaks out and shuts down areas of your brain, or fails to make it to important areas of your brain and **KILLS** sections of it off. Not nice. Strokes can leave you unable to move, talk, or walk. Although there are many possible causes for strokes, studies have shown that if you drink heavily, you are more likely to suffer from one.

5. Alcoholism

Some people become **addicted** to booze. They don't drink just because it tastes nice or they enjoy it. They drink because they have to, because they can't get up in the morning without a drink, they can't leave their house without a drink, they can't function without a drink. Alcoholism is a **very serious problem** that can lead to all kinds of medical conditions and depression and, in severe cases, death.

In most cases, alcoholism creeps up on you and overtakes you. That's why no one should ever get drunk because they think it solves a problem, makes life easier, or makes bad things go away. It doesn't. No matter what your worries or problems are, they will still be around after you have sobered up. It's worth realizing that research shows the drinking patterns we have as teenagers tend to be the drinking patterns we keep for the rest of our lives.

Get into the habit of drinking so much you throw up now, and you'll probably do it for many, many years to come.

There is nothing wrong with drinking in and of itself. It tastes nice. It's social. Adults do it all the time. But . . .

There *is* something wrong with drinking so much that you pass out, throw up, or can't remember what you did while you where drunk.

There *is* something wrong with drinking because you can't face a problem or because you think when you are drunk you are a better or nicer person.

When it comes to drinking, always remember that moderation and self-control are the keys.

Cigarettes

Butts, smokes!

They might not be illegal if you are over eighteen, but cigarettes can and do kill.

Smoking is a disgusting habit that only ever leads to bad and unpleasant side effects, from the purely cosmetic:

STAINED FINGERS,

smelly clothes,

poor skin, and

YELLOW TEETH,

to the terminal: heart disease, thrombosis, and lung cancer.

Why do it?

Well, smoking can relax some people, making them feel more sociable and at ease. And some teenagers think it's cool and rebellious.

But why?

What is so cool about **smelling like an ashtray,** and what's so rebellious about **COUGHING UP GREEN SLIME** every morning?

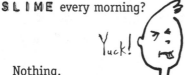

Nothing.

However, smoking among teenagers is on the increase. It comes down to that old problem of peer pressure. Ironically, the first time you smoke a cigarette, it will taste disgusting. It might even make you throw up, but odds are you'll stand there with your friends, feeling awful, your eyes watering, and say something like, "Mmmm, smooth."

But of course it's not.

Unfortunately, smoking is highly addictive, and any of the temporary pleasures that you gain from having a cigarette are very quickly replaced by a craving for more and more.

115

Ask any smoker who has been smoking for a number of years whether they would like to quit, and almost all will say yes. Ask them why they don't and they will more often than not say that they can't.

It's just best not to start.

Man! We really are getting into the heavy stuff!

Drugs

There are a lot of drugs out there, and if you go to clubs or parties or just hang out, it's more than likely that you will be offered some form of illegal drug.

If you are wondering what is meant by illegal drugs, well, they include, to name the most common:

Whoa!

ecstasy, *cocaine,* **MARIJUANA,** *speed,* **LSD,** and **HEROIN**.

Ultimately, no one can stop you from taking and experimenting with drugs.

However, all of the above drugs are illegal for a reason: They do varying degrees of harm to your body, and they impair your ability to make smart decisions.

Don't believe all the talk about some drugs making you happy all the time or giving you an insight into the meaning of life or being good for your soul.

They're not.

They give you a quick pulse of pleasure and then can leave you feeling crappy for a long time. And, in the worst cases, they can leave you dead.

IS THAT A RISK THAT YOU WANT TO TAKE?

But if you do get into the situation where you decide to experiment with drugs, just stop for a minute and think . . .

- *Are you being pushed into it by peer pressure?*
- *Are you doing it because all your friends are doing it?*
- *Or because you think it will make you look cool?*
- *Or because you think you have to because it's that type of party?*
- *Or because you don't think you'll have a good time unless you do?*
- *Or because you think it's fun to try anything once?*

None of these reasons is good enough.

So, what's out there?

Inhalants

When inhaled, certain glues, deodorants, and aerosols create a floating, empty feeling. These are not strictly drugs and not illegal to buy, but they can do serious damage to your lungs, heart, brain, liver, and kidneys that sometimes causes death. The biggest danger of inhaling any form of glue or gas is that it's very difficult to regulate how much you are taking in, so it's very easy to overdose.

Marijuana

{aka weed, pot, hash, grass, ganja}

Using marijuana, which either comes in a resin or in an herb-like state, produces different effects on different people. It usually makes people feel relaxed, warm, and sociable, but it can also produce feelings of

ANXIETY, paranoia, and panic.

Although the long-term effects of marijuana aren't really understood, it's believed that it can spark off underlying mental health problems, slow the reflexes, and produce hallucinations.

Speed

{aka billy, wiz, crank}

Speed is a powerful stimulant that increases the heart rate and body temperature while removing the need for food or sleep. And while it can make people feel alert, communicative, and talkative, it can also result in drastic mood swings, irritability, and restlessness.

Ecstasy

{aka E, X, MDMA}

Ecstasy is one of the major influences in youth and dance culture. It's sometimes simply called E and comes in a small papery tablet.

It's associated with heightened perceptions and an overall feeling of warmth and happiness.

However, the combination of ecstasy and overheated clubs can cause massive dehydration and heatstroke, and it's not unknown for people to collapse after taking an ecstasy tablet.

Studies have also indicated that ecstasy affects both the brain cells and the liver, causing long-term damage if the drug is used regularly. Also, after taking ecstasy, users often experience a period of depression and listlessness.

Cocaine

{aka coke, charlie, horse, snow, blow}

Cocaine is a white powdery substance that, when snorted into the nose or smoked, can boost feelings of excitement and confidence.

However, regular use of cocaine creates major heart and digestive problems. It's also linked to paranoia, irritability, and aggression.

Cocaine as well as crack, a stronger form of cocaine, are highly addictive and can lead to both social and financial difficulties, as the addict will do anything to get more.

LSD

{aka acid}

LSD is similar to ecstasy in appearance. It's also a chemical-based drug that comes in small papery tablets.

Unlike ecstasy, it is a hallucinogen, which means that it can induce strange and disturbing visions. This is known as a trip. However, sometimes these trips can be extremely unpleasant and very scary — not unlike the worst and most believable **nightmare** that you've ever had. And once your trip has started, you can't stop it until the drug has run its course. Prolonged use can also lead to disturbing flashbacks that may occur years after taking the drug.

Heroin

{aka junk, horse}
Heroin is **FIERCELY ADDICTIVE.** It is either smoked, snorted, or injected directly into the bloodstream, and due to the sharing of dirty needles, it can contribute to the spread of HIV and AIDS. A temporary feeling of elation and extreme tranquility is rapidly replaced by a desperate craving for more heroin, as well as by cramps, fevers, and paranoia.

All forms of illegal drugs carry a heavy price for their use. If you are a minor you can get detention in a Department of Youth Services facility and probation. If you are seventeen, eighteen, or older you can receive anywhere from two and a half to ten years in prison for possession and anywhere from two and a half to twenty years for selling drugs. But it's not just a legal price.

The brief pleasant sensations that all drugs create can leave you feeling like you want more of that quick high. Every time you use a drug, the downtime of depression, paranoia, and panic gets longer, and the good feelings get shorter. So it's not unusual to find yourself caught in a DOWNWARD SPIRAL

of greater and greater use of more and more dangerous types of drugs.

And always remember: Because drugs are illegal, people from whom you obtain drugs are involved in criminal activity and are probably not to be trusted. One of the great dangers of drugs is that you might not get exactly what you think you are getting but rather an even more dangerous mixture.

It is also impossible to control your behavior under the influence of drugs and/or alcohol. You can end up making bad decisions, such as trying to drive a car while you're high, that can lead to serious injuries and even death for you and your friends. Is that really a price you are willing to pay? **THINK ABOUT IT.**

Fights

The way you act around other guys can be heavily influenced by what your friends think and do.

It feels good to be part of a gang or a clique, to be surrounded by your friends and to feel their support when you get into a difficult situation.

It has to do with safety: safety in numbers, safety in a group.

One for all and all for one.

Unfortunately, groups can have a downside. If you've ever gotten into a fight, you know that it's usually all the people around the outside of the fight — often your friends — who are doing all the cheering and encouraging.

They're the ones who are trying to get the fight going and make sure that the two people involved start slinging punches, which is odd — because if they were such good friends, they'd try to stop you from getting hurt.

So, why don't they?

Well, as a guy, it's still seen as an act of courage to get into a fight, to square up to someone and punch their lights out or, if necessary, take a few punches yourself.

But why?

Because that's what real guys do — isn't it?

What's the point?

Usually if two people get into a fight, it's over something really stupid and small. How many times have you heard someone say:

"He looked at me funny."

"I don't like his pants."

"He said something about my mother."

Are they good enough reasons to square up and get physical with someone?

Not really.

Fighting

No one who gets into a fight really wants to be there.
Who would?

You might get hurt, and no matter how tough you might like to think you are, no one wants to go to school on Monday morning with a black eye.

You can't flirt with a black eye!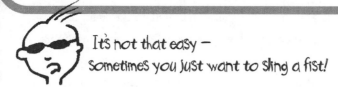

Also, if after a fight you ask the two guys who were going at it tooth and nail a couple of minutes earlier what all the big fuss was about, they'll probably not be able to tell you.

Why?

Because the fight has become more important than the initial argument.

So, why don't you just laugh off the fight, maybe shoot a few angry glances at the other guy, and walk away?

 It's not that easy —
Sometimes you just want to sling a fist!

Because once you've gotten into that situation, where a fight might be in the air, your so-called friends tend to start egging you on.

Who said
Something about
my mother?

"Did you hear what he just said about your mother?"

123

Sound familiar?

It's almost as if you don't have a say in the matter, isn't it?

But you do.

You don't have to do anything that you don't want to do. Even if your friends are trying to encourage you to start a fight, you can always walk away.

In fact, it takes more courage to walk away from a fight than it does to start one.

So, that's one thing.

But what if someone squares up to you and decides that *he* wants to have a fight?

Surely then you haven't got any choice — it's a matter of self-defense, right? Well, yes and no.

If another guy starts **_getting aggressive,_**

GETTING IN YOUR FACE, POKING YOUR SHOULDER,

and **GENERALLY "ASKING FOR IT,"** you might think that is justification for making the first move. You could catch him off guard and land him one on the chin. But then you haven't achieved anything. You've just gotten yourself into a fight that you didn't want to start in the first place, but now, because you made the first move, you've got to finish it.

So, what could you do instead?

Simply walk away.

TURN AROUND AND WALK AWAY.

The guy who's picking a fight with you will probably do everything he possibly can to try to provoke you. He'll call you a coward, he'll try and start getting physical with you, and he might even punch you.

But just like dancing cheek-to-cheek and making love, fighting takes two people to make it work.

If you simply refuse to get into a fight, the fight won't happen.

Don't say a word,
don't get into name-calling
or a shouting match,
don't rise to the bait —
just pick your stuff up
and walk away.

That's quite a tough-guy thing to do!

To be able to walk away from a fight, you have to be strong.
You might feel like
a coward,
you might feel like
a chicken,
and you might feel that you are running away.

But you're not.

It takes **huge** amounts of courage to walk away from a confrontation even though you know you might GET MORE RESPECT FROM YOUR FRIENDS and more short-term glory from getting into a fight.

It's a bit of an old cliché from Saturday afternoon Westerns, but the guy who refuses to fight, even if he gets punched a couple of times, his ego gets bruised, or he gets a black eye, is still the winner.

Bullying

Don't think bullying is just something that happens at elementary school with little kids stealing each other's lunch money.

It's a problem that happens throughout life and can cause misery for the person who is being bullied.

But what is bullying?

Well, it's picking on someone because he is different from you or your friends.

- *It might be because he is smarter than you.*
  Or not as smart.
- *It might be because he doesn't have as many friends.*
  Or has more friends.
- *It might be because he is disabled.*
  Or zitty. Or dresses differently.
- *It might be because he is of a different race or ethnic background.*
  In which case it's called racism.
- *It might be because he is effeminate or gay.*
  In which case it's called homophobia.

It can be for any reason — but whatever the reason is, there is absolutely no excuse for being a bully.

Bullying is based on ignorance and fear, it's based on stupidity and prejudice, and it's based on the "that person is different from me and my friends; he must be weird" syndrome.

If You're a Bully

So, how do you stop yourself from bullying or becoming a bully?

There is one very simple way.

Next time you and your friends are teasing someone, calling him names, or generally making his life less than pleasant — **JUST STOP.**

Stop and think how you would like it if it was you or your best friend or your brother being picked on, being made to feel like you didn't belong, like you were a bit of a freak. Just stop and think how isolated and scared you might feel, how alone and desperate.

Stop bullying someone, stop making his life miserable, and give him back his self-respect. You had no right to take it away from him in the first place.

Bullying

Here's a question: What's the difference between bullying someone and teasing him? Answer: Absolutely nothing if every time you see someone you tease him.

No one minds being ribbed or the butt of a joke from time to time, but if you are always making someone the punch line of a gag, you are bullying him.

It's strange, but sometimes bullies don't realize they are bullying someone — they usually just think they are having fun and the only reason their victim is getting upset is because he doesn't have a sense of humor.

But they're wrong.

Being Bullied

Unfortunately, it's not as simple to deal with *being* bullied. If someone is bullying you, it can make your life hell.

- *You don't want to get up in the morning.*
- *You don't want to go to school.*
- *You don't want to go out.*
- *You feel worthless, isolated, and weird.*
- *You begin to believe the bully's chants. If you get called Stinky enough times, you will begin to believe that you smell, even when you don't.*

So, what can you do if you are being bullied?

Well, you could try standing up to the bully — but unfortunately, that rarely works. The bully is either part of a gang and so he has safety in numbers or, like most bullies, he's been clever enough to pick on you only when he knows you can't fight back.

A better tactic is not to try to get even, but instead to go talk to someone about it. Your mom and dad, a teacher — anyone older than the bully who is in a position of authority and can do something to stop his antisocial behavior would do.

Or talk to your friends.

Never think that just because you are telling someone else about the fact that you are being bullied, it somehow makes you a wimp or a coward. It's almost impossible to deal with the situation yourself.

Bullies are smart, because they often pick only on people who can't retaliate, either because the bully is much older than they are or because the bully holds a position of power over them.

But really, bullies are picking on you only because they feel insecure about themselves.

Bullies are weak cowards and deserve no respect.

It's not your fault that someone is bullying you.

YOU DON'T HAVE THE PROBLEM — HE DOES.

He's the one who is being antisocial and unpleasant.

It's easy to say — though much less easy to do — but don't ever let a bully get you down.

SO, NOW WHAT?

How you live your life is all up to you.
But always remember these five things:

1. Puberty is a roller-coaster ride. Sometimes the best policy is to just hang on and close your eyes. From shaving to girls to masturbating to feeling depressed, things can seem confusing. But your body knows what's going on — trust it.

Keep in mind that once you become an adult, things don't necessarily get easier or simpler. You don't hit twenty and suddenly have all the answers. But the challenging experiences you go through during puberty will help prepare you for the rest of your life.

Roller-coaster rides make me blow chunks!

3. Remember that you are not alone. Every guy your age is going through the same things you are, and every adult male you know also went through them when he was younger. So, don't be afraid to talk to friends, family, teachers, coaches, or counselors about any of the stuff you are feeling — chances are, they'll know just what you're talking about and will want to help.

4. There is no one else exactly like you anywhere in the world. It's cool to be YOU.

Oh, I guess there is no number five.

What a rip-off!

Resources

HELP! PLACES TO CALL, BOOKS TO READ, WEBSITES TO CHECK OUT.

You've heard the expression "No man is an island"? Well, that goes for guys, too. It means that sometimes you can't go it alone. Sometimes you need *additional support* — SOMEONE TO LEAN ON, *a shoulder to cry on,* a person to listen, or some MORE INFORMATION before you make an important decision. Here are some organizations that might be able to help:

Chapter One

Surviving Love and Sex

STDs

Centers for Disease Control National STD & AIDS Hotlines
1-800-CDC-INFO (232-4636)
TTY: 1-888-232-6348
www.cdc.gov

Being Gay

American Veterans for Equal Rights (AVER)
www.aver.us

National Gay and Lesbian Task Force
Washington, DC office:
1325 Massachusetts Avenue NW, Suite 600
Washington, DC 20005
202-393-5177
Fax: 202-393-2241
www.thetaskforce.org

Parents, Families and Friends of Lesbians and Gays (PFLAG)
PFLAG National Office
1828 L Street, NW, Suite 660
Washington, DC 20036
202-467-8180
Fax: 202-349-0788
E-mail: info@pflag.org
www.pflag.org

Chapter Two

Surviving All the Changes in Your Body

Adolescent Directory on Line (ADOL)
**http://site.educ.indiana.edu/aboutus/
AdolescenceDirectoryonLineADOL/tabid/
4785/Default.aspx**
Check out this Web site for information on adolescent issues such as teen violence, attention-deficit hyperactivity disorder, eating disorders, depression, alcohol, drugs, AIDS, sexuality, acne, and much more.

The "What's Happening to My Body?" Book for Boys
by Lynda Madaras with Area Madaras
(Newmarket Press)
This book covers the body's changing size and shape, the growth spurt, reproductive organs, perspiration and pimples, as well as AIDS, STDs, and birth control.

Chapter Three

Surviving Teenage Ups and Downs

Boys & Girls Clubs of America
National Headquarters
1275 Peachtree Street NE
Atlanta, GA 30309-3506
404-487-5700
E-mail: info@bgca.org
www.bgca.org

Horizons Youth Services
3586 Horizons Way
Harrisonburg, VA 22802
540-896-9947
Fax: 540-896-3548
www.horizonsyouthservices.com

National Center for Missing & Exploited Children
Charles B. Wang International Children's Building
699 Prince Street
Alexandria, Virginia 22314-3175
1-800-THE-LOST (843-5678)
Fax: 703-224-2122
www.missingkids.com

National Runaway Switchboard
3080 N. Lincoln Avenue
Chicago, IL 60657
1-800-RUNAWAY (786-2929)
Business office:
773-880-9860
Fax: 773-929-5150
www.1800runaway.org

National Youth Crisis Hotline
1-800-442-HOPE (4673)
A twenty-four-hour crisis line for any crisis—from pregnancy to drugs to depression.

Teen Education and Crisis Hotline
1-800-273-TALK (8255)
www.teachhotline.org

Chapter Four

Surviving Teenage Social Life

Alateen
1600 Corporate Landing Parkway
Virginia Beach, VA 23454-5617
757-563-1600
Fax: 757-563-1655
www.al-anon.alateen.org
For teenagers affected by alcoholism.

Cocaine Hotline
1-800-NODRUGS (663-7847)
877-456-3313
Counseling and referrals.

The Coroner's Report
P.O. Box 1932
North Little Rock, AR 72115
Phone: 501-940-GANG (4264)
E-mail: Steve@gangwar.com
www.gangwar.com
Lots of information about gangs, why they are popular, and why to stay away from them.

D.A.R.E.
Drug Abuse Resistance Education
9800 La Cienega Boulevard, Suite 401
Inglewood, CA 90301
1-800-223-DARE (3273)
Fax: 310-215-0180
E-mail: webmaster@dare.org
www.dare.org

National Association for Children of Alcoholics
10920 Connecticut Avenue, Suite 100
Kensington, Maryland 20895
888-55-4COAS (554-2627)
301-468-0985
Fax: 301-468-0987
E-mail: nacoa@nacoa.org
www.nacoa.org

National Families in Action
2957 Clairmont Road NE, Suite 150
Atlanta, Georgia 30329
404-248-9676
Fax: 404-248-1312
E-mail: nfia@nationalfamilies.org
www.nationalfamilies.org
Provides accurate drug information to parents and teens.

S.A.D.A.
Students Against Drugs and Alcohol
918-231-8313
www.sada.org
Substance abuse educational program for public and private schools, churches, and youth groups, with school assembly speakers and drug awareness seminars.

SADD
Students Against Destructive Decisions
SADD National
255 Main Street
Marlborough, MA 01752
1-877-SADD-INC (723-3462)
Fax: 508-481-5759
E-mail: info@sadd.org
www.sadd.org

Teen Health and the Media
University of Washington
Experimental Education Unit
Box 357925
Seattle, WA 98195
206-543-9414
888-TEEN-NET (833-6638)
E-mail: thmedia@u.washington.edu
http://depts.washington.edu/thmedia/
Teens talking to teens about healthy choices in the areas of substance abuse prevention, tobacco, nutrition, sexuality, pregnancy prevention, and injury and suicide prevention.

Youth-to-Youth International
547 E. 11th Avenue
Columbus, OH 43211
614-224-4506
Fax: 614-224-8451
E-mail: y2yinfo@compdrug.org
www.youthtoyouth.net

ACKNOWLEDGMENTS

There are so many people who have helped with this book that to name them all would be impossible. However, thank you: **Mum and Dad** — it's only because you did such a great job that I can write a book like this. **Stephen**, for being the best brother and a dear friend. **Nick**, for knowing when a beer is more important than a deadline. (Always.) **Ruth and Brenda**, for knowing when a deadline is more important than a beer. (Always.) **Catherine**, for her uncanny knowledge and understanding of young boys. **Greg at the BBC**, for friendship, wise words, and employment. **Matthew at LWT**, for never letting me get away with things I shouldn't. **Eileen**, for Muppet dancing above and beyond the call of duty. **Alan Remy at the *Daily Record***, my boss for five years at the best newspaper in the world. **The Live and Kicking girls — Lucy, Annette, and Suzanne.** "Another bottle of red, girls?"

 JEREMY DALDRY was born in 1969. He has worked as a freelance writer for a number of publications, including *GQ*, as well as several television shows. He lives in London with a classic car that doesn't work, a guitar he can't play, and a signed picture of Groucho Marx.